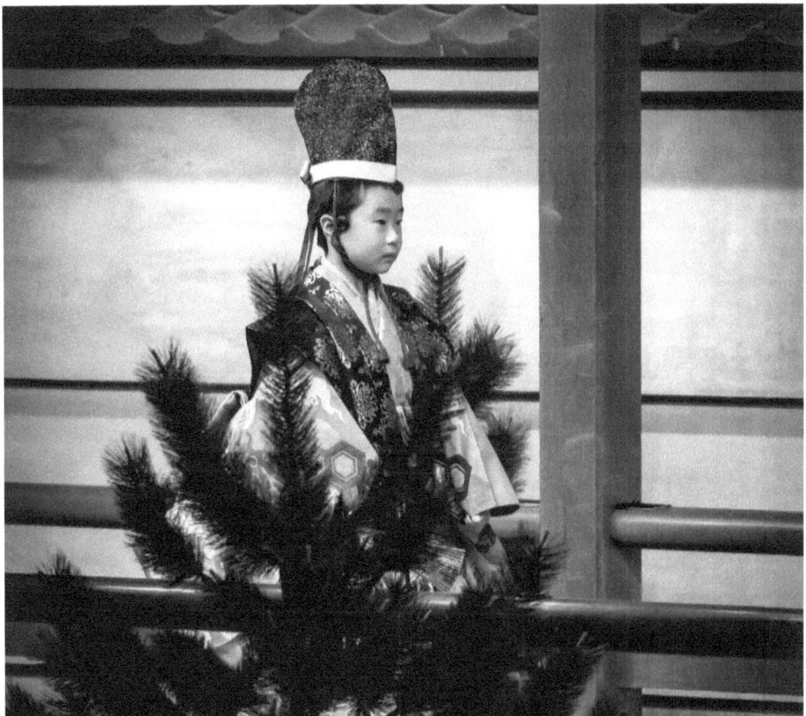

The text of this book has been entirely imagined
without any interviews

Translation : Jun Tsutsumi

The Little Yoshitsune

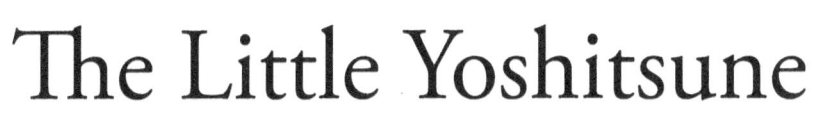

REHEARSAL
AT MY MASTER'S PLACE

When
I grow
up, I
will be
a noh
master.

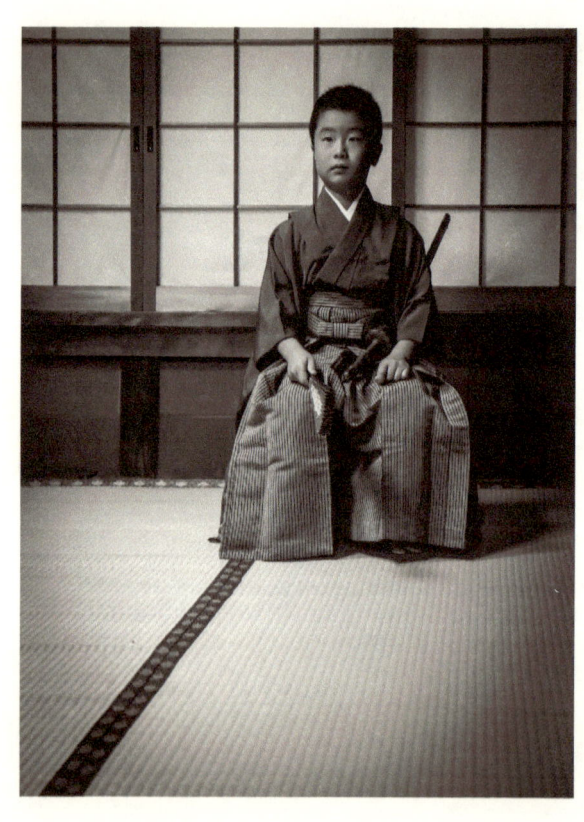

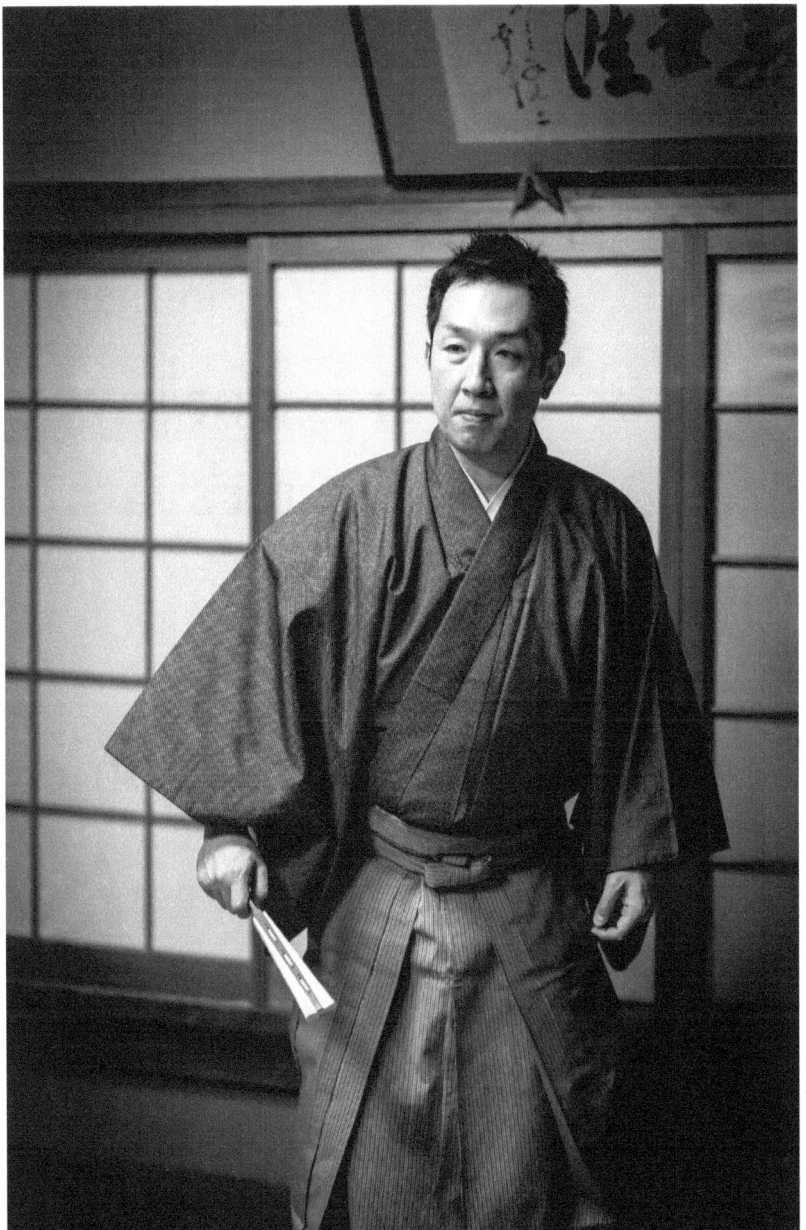

My noh master is not my dad. And my master's father was not a noh master.

Today, anyone can become a noh master.

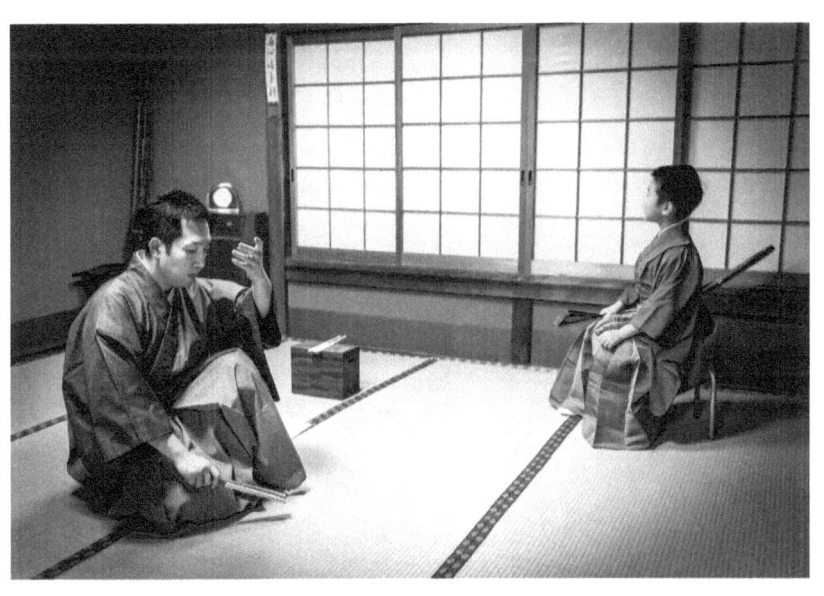

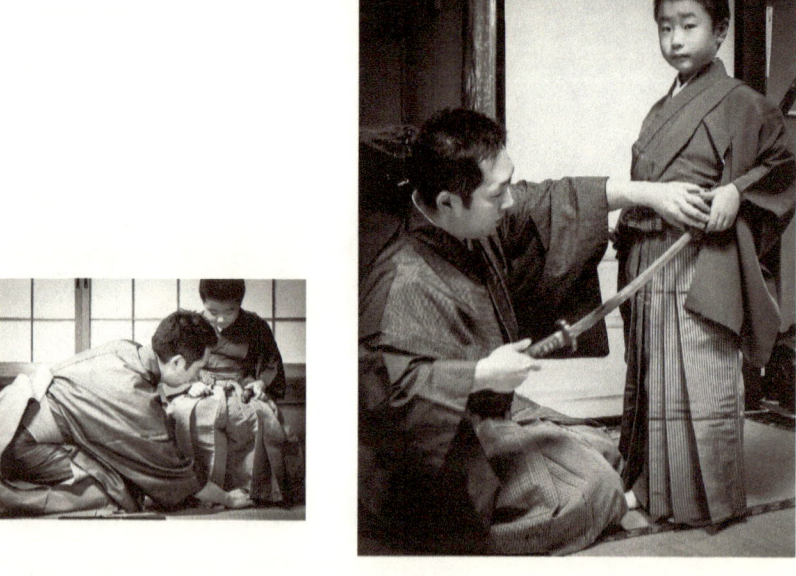

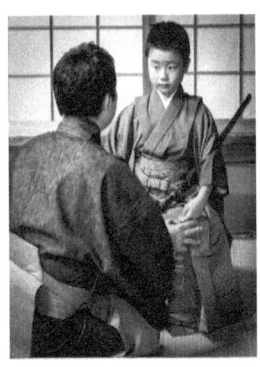

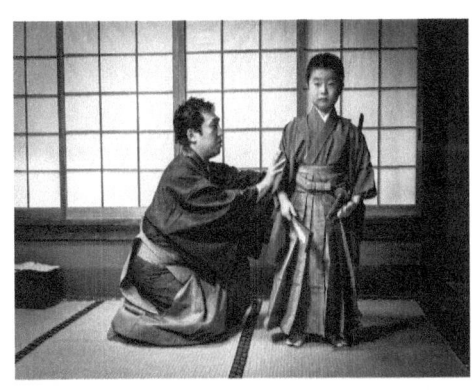

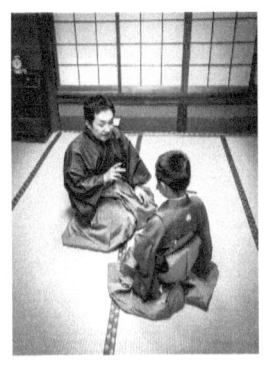

My master is kind. He pays attention to me and explains everything.

Some noh masters look stern and make me feel scared. But not him.

He's a school friend of my mom.

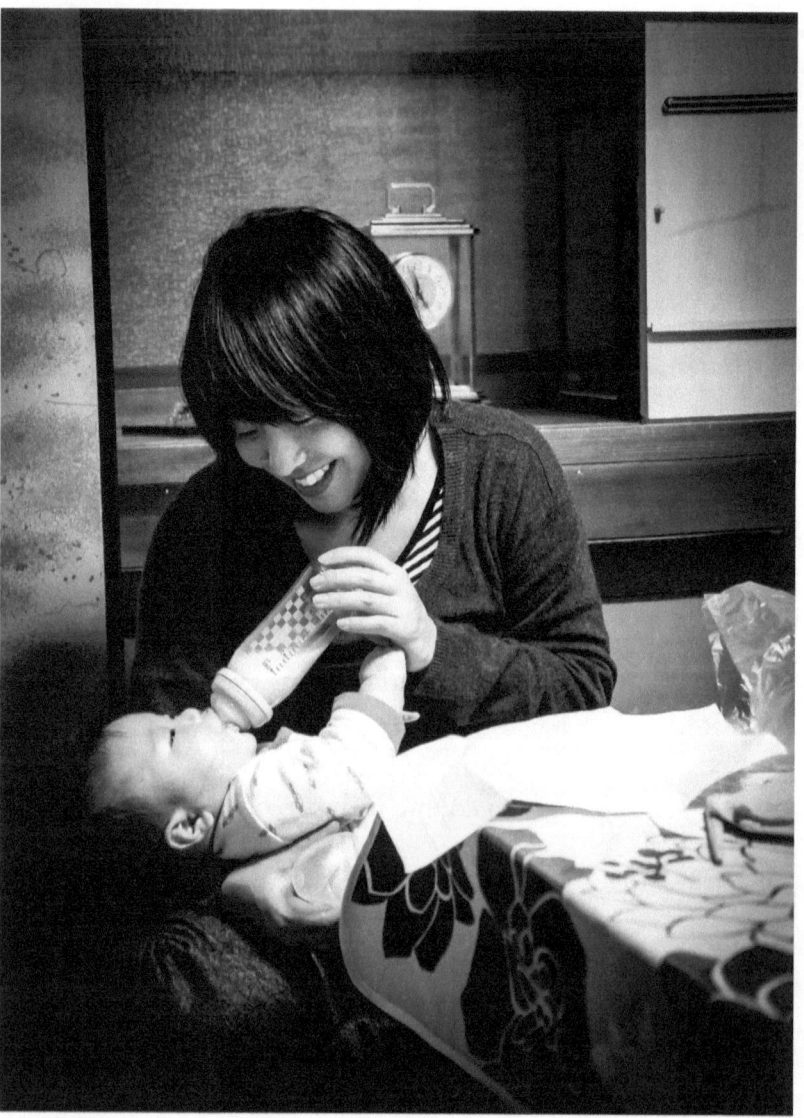

When my mom explained to me what noh was about, she told me that I would be a samurai with a sword, a great warrior, the greatest samurai of all time.

So I said yes.

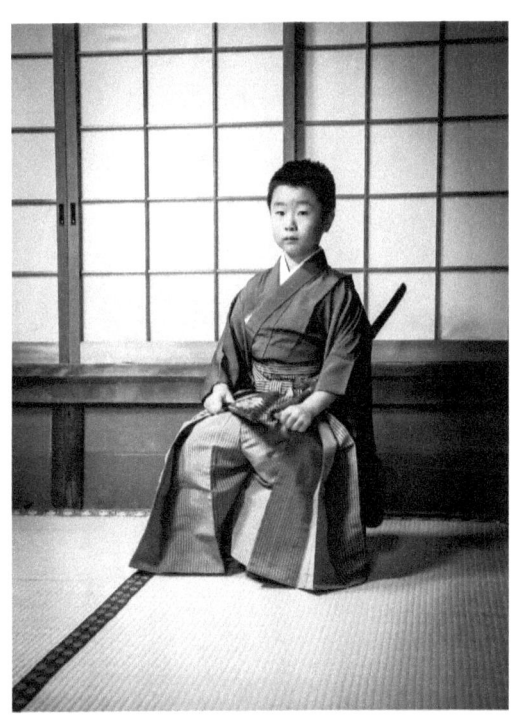

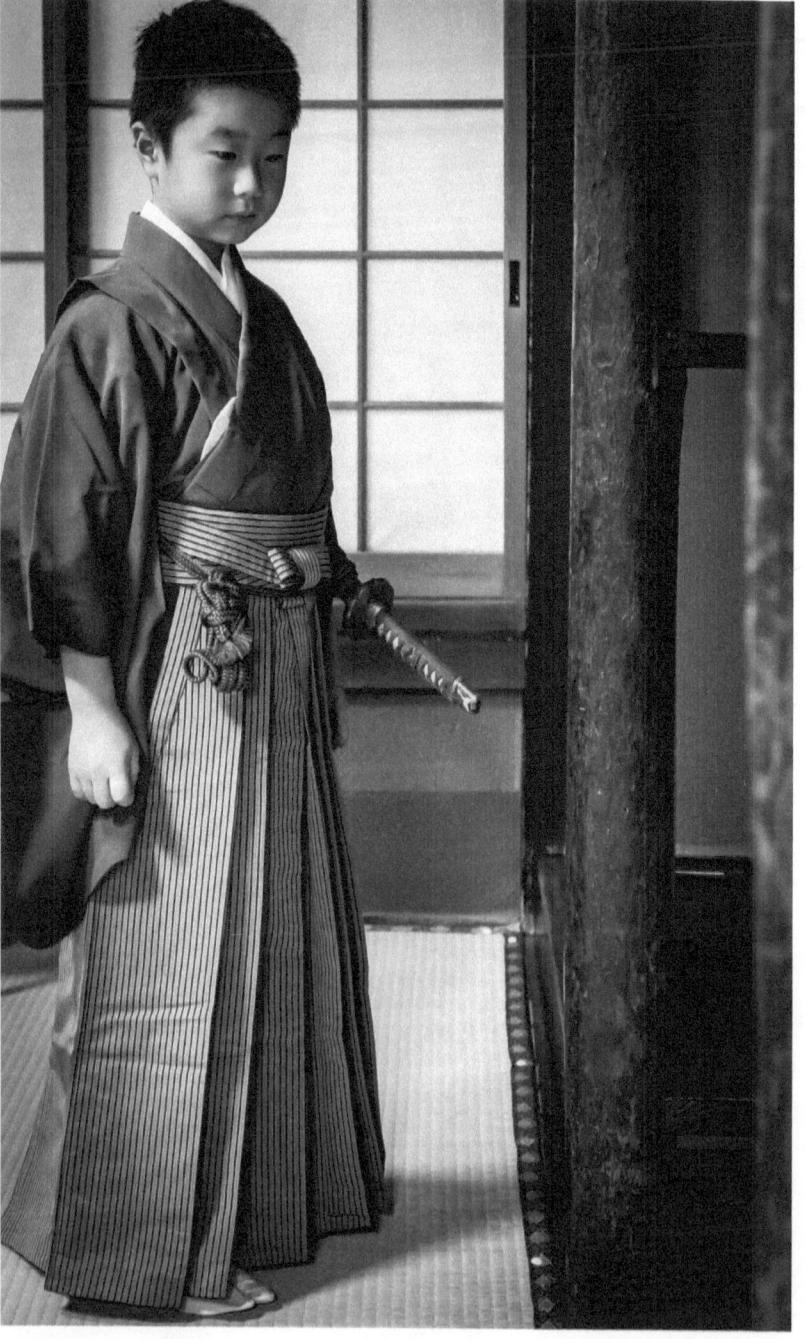

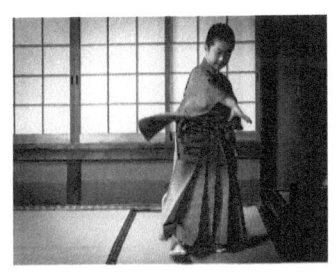

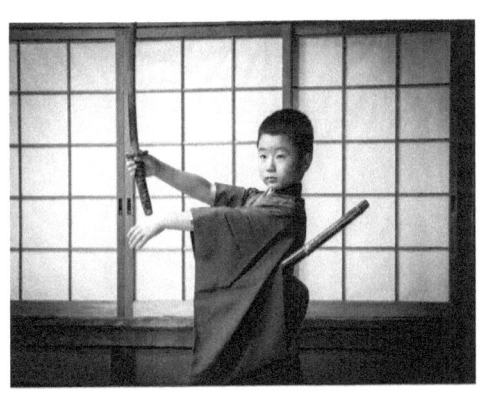

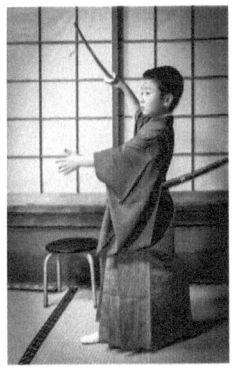

I like to play
the strongest
of all samurai.

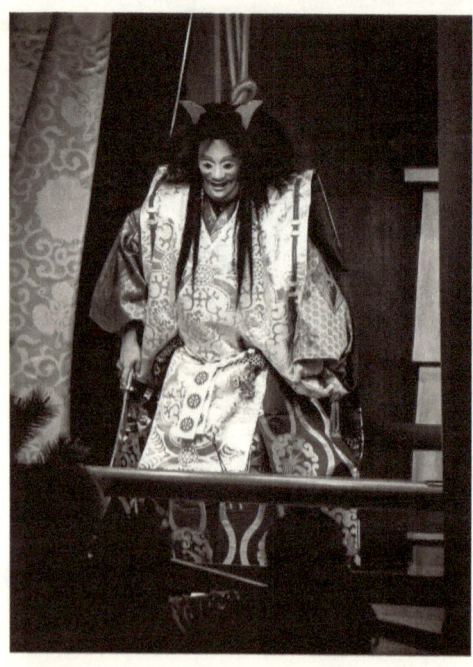

I would not want to be a demon. Or a girl.

In the play, my master plays a mean ghost AND a girl.

It doesn't seem to bother him.

I find it weird.

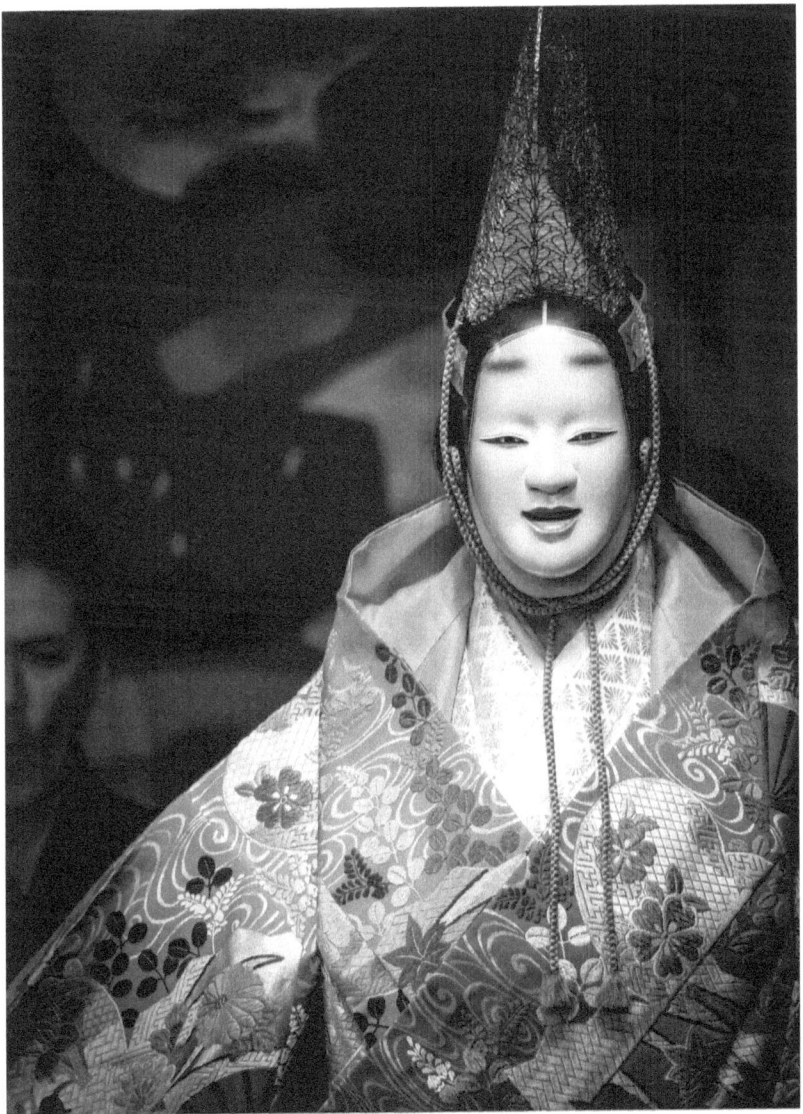

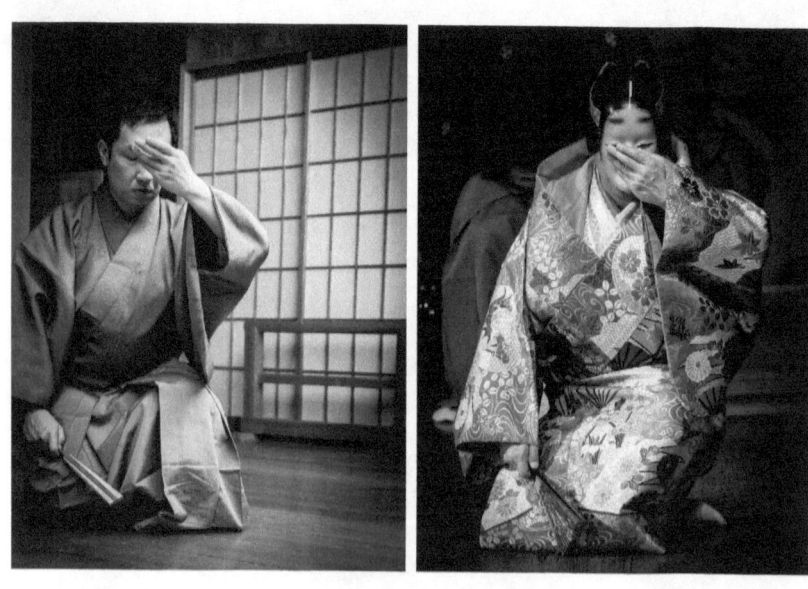

A girl can cry easily.

A boy should not cry.

Here, if I'm crying, it's because it really hurt.

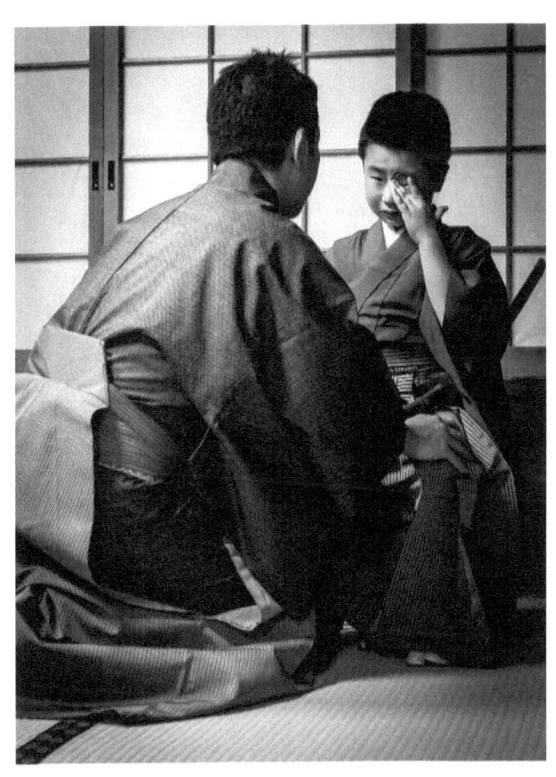

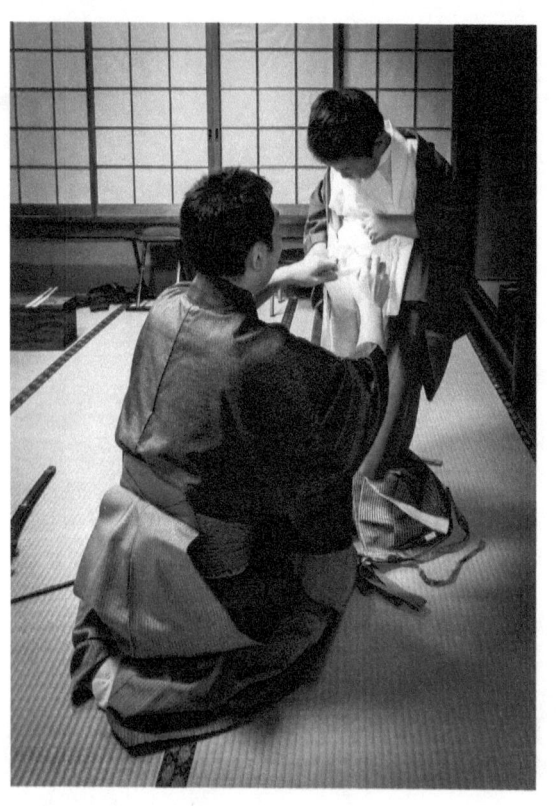
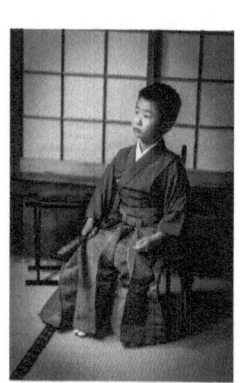

I tried to hold it in as much as I could. But one of the strings under my belt was too tight. I couldn't breathe when I sat.

I didn't say anything. To show that I am brave. Like Yoshitsune.

On the day of the performance, we'll be careful about the string.

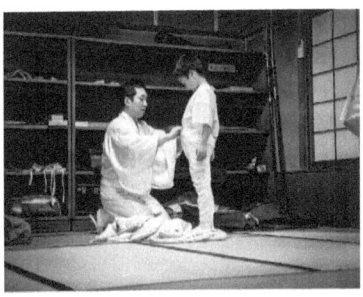

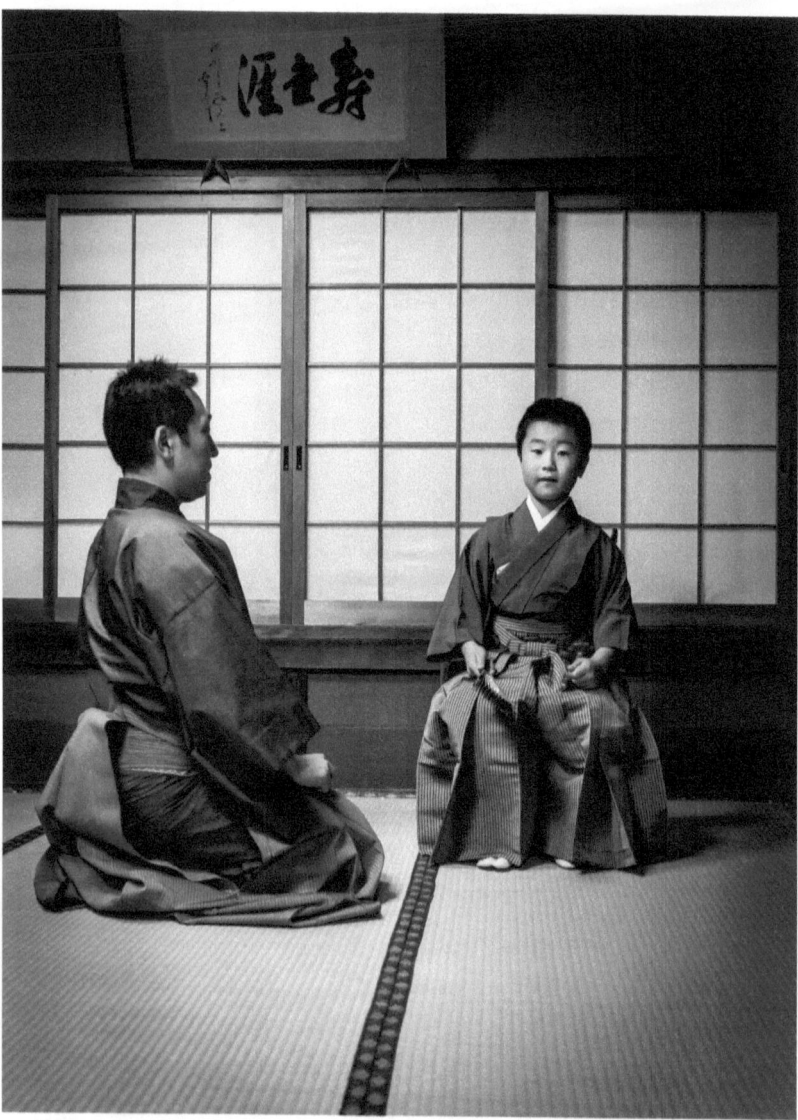

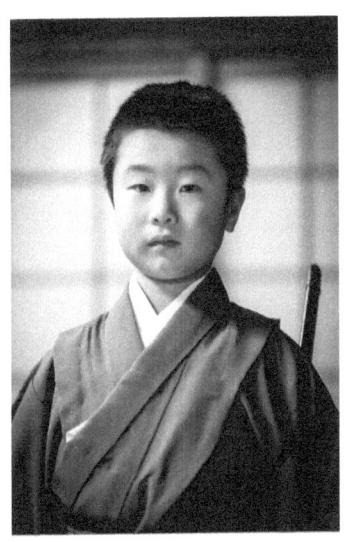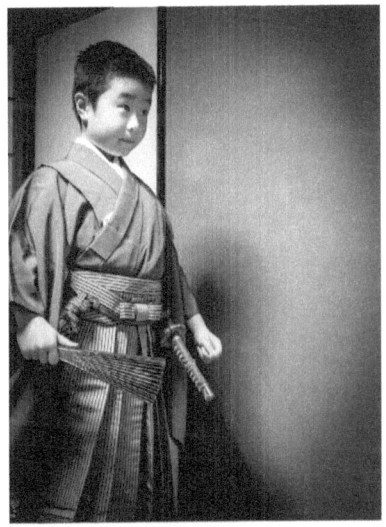

I like to wear a kimono on the tatami in the washitsu of my master. It's too bad we don't live like this anymore. I've thought hard about it and don't know why we don't. It's more beautiful.

I love noh because everyone behaves like lords with each other.

In the play, I'm the Prince. My master's character has to respect me.

But after the lesson, I bow to him and thank him with the same respect.

In the world of noh, we bow and thank each other like lords. We feel noble when we do this.

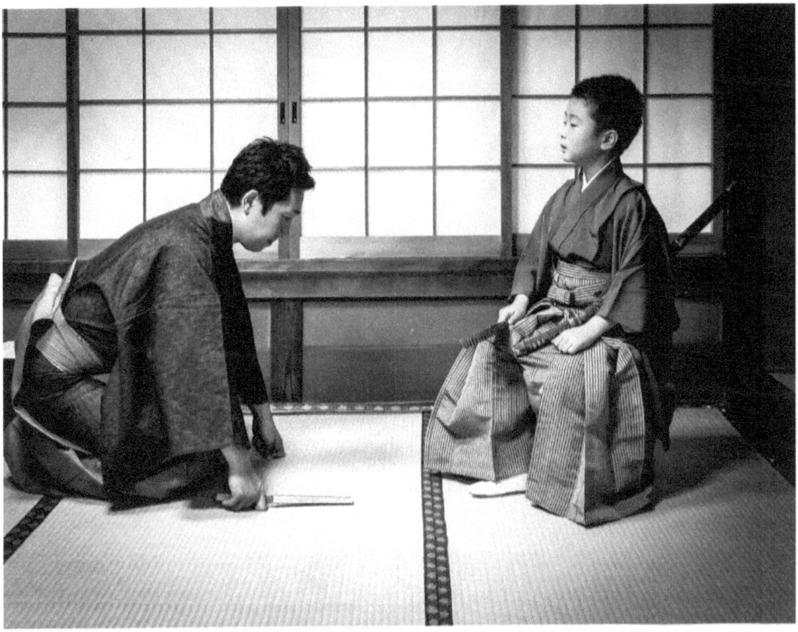

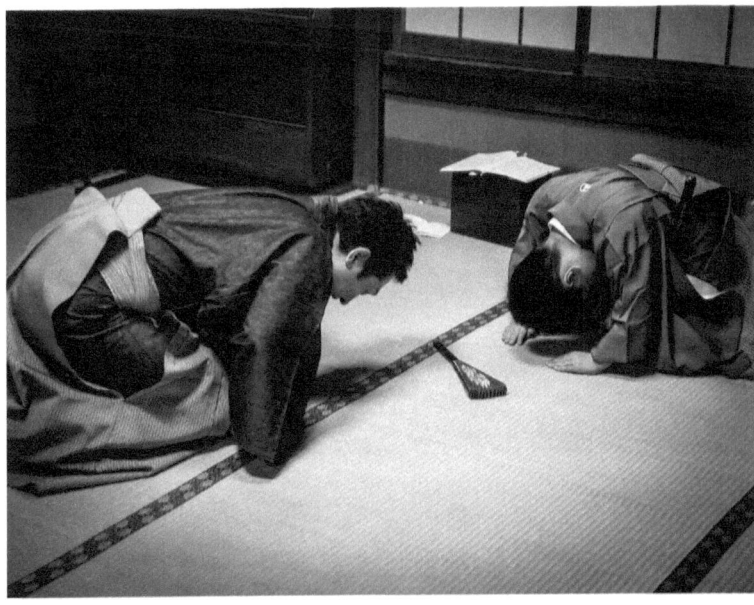

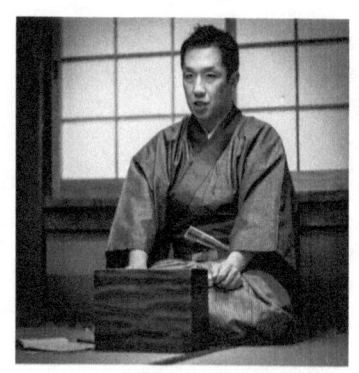

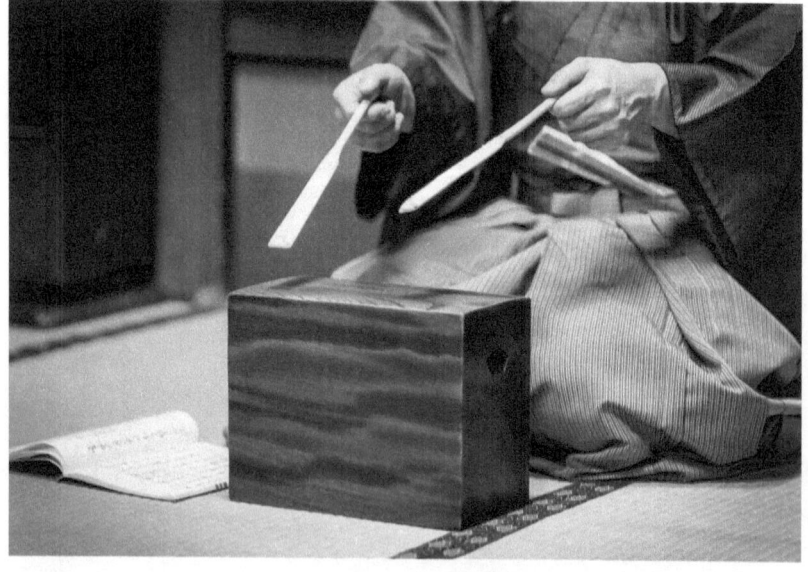

My master is really amazing. He knows how to do everything.

Sing with a deep and powerful voice.
Shout the cries of the kakegoe who can be funny, scary, and sometimes sad.
Stay seated in seiza for more than an hour without moving.
Jump really high while dancing.
Put on kimonos and fold them away in seconds.
Fight with a sword and a spear.
He knows the whole play by heart! My mom told me he knows dozens of pieces by heart! I wish I had the same memory for school! He can also explain the stories. And he gets along well with the other noh masters.

When we rehearse at home, I like when he taps on his wooden block that he uses as the hip drum. I learned that this drum hurts your fingers so much that it's usually only used on the day of the play. Now I hear the drum differently...

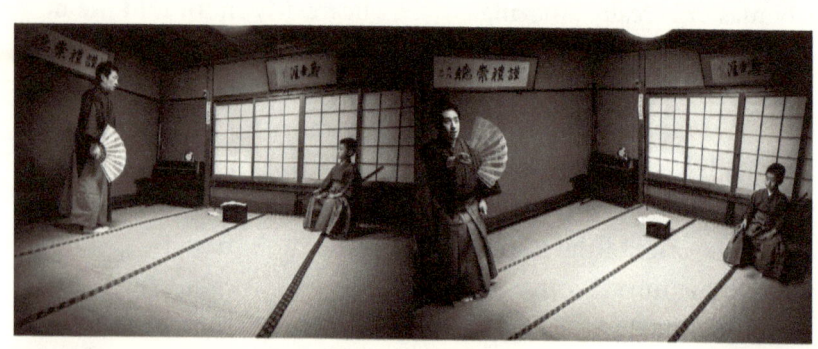

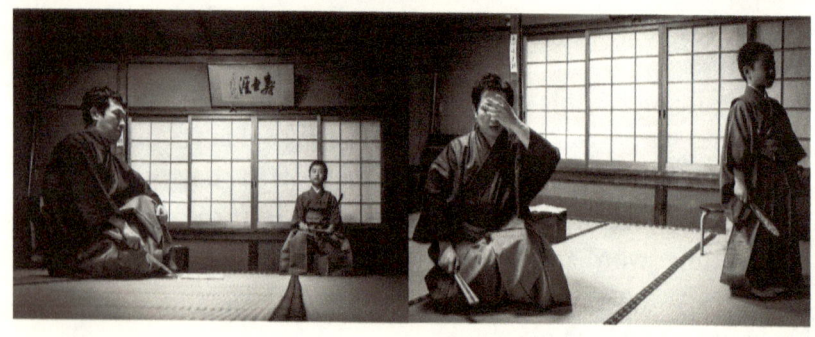

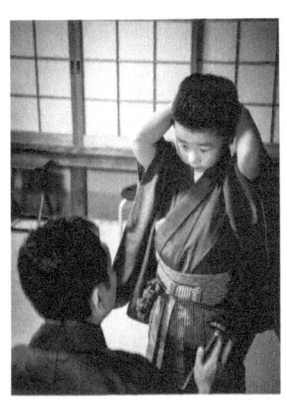

Sometimes noh is
slow and I'm bored.

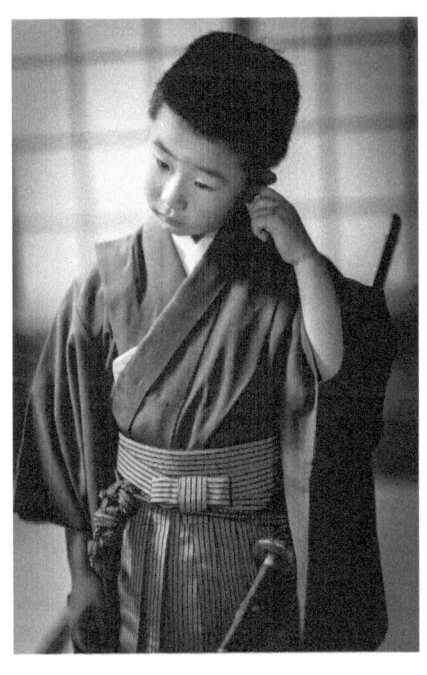

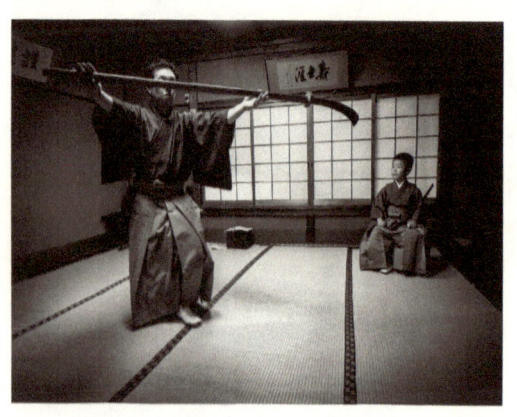

And sometimes it's so fast that I don't have time to see every-thing.

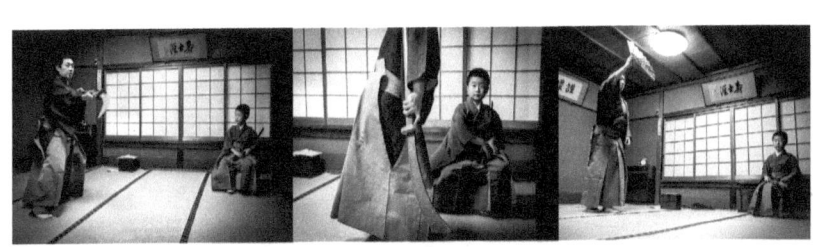

As soon as the rehearsal is over, I change and the master folds the kimono like an origami in two minutes.

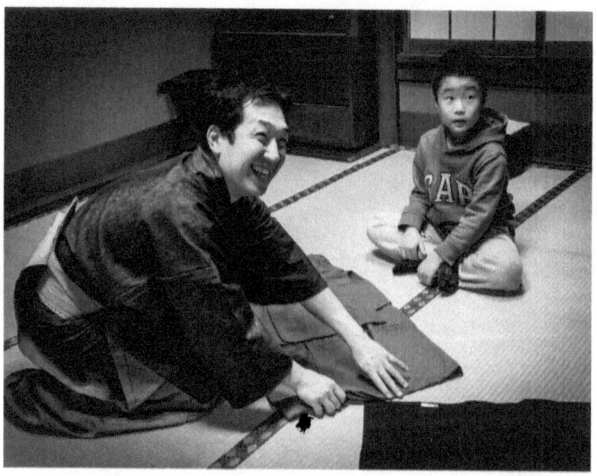

Japan must have been beautiful when everyone always wore kimonos, even children…

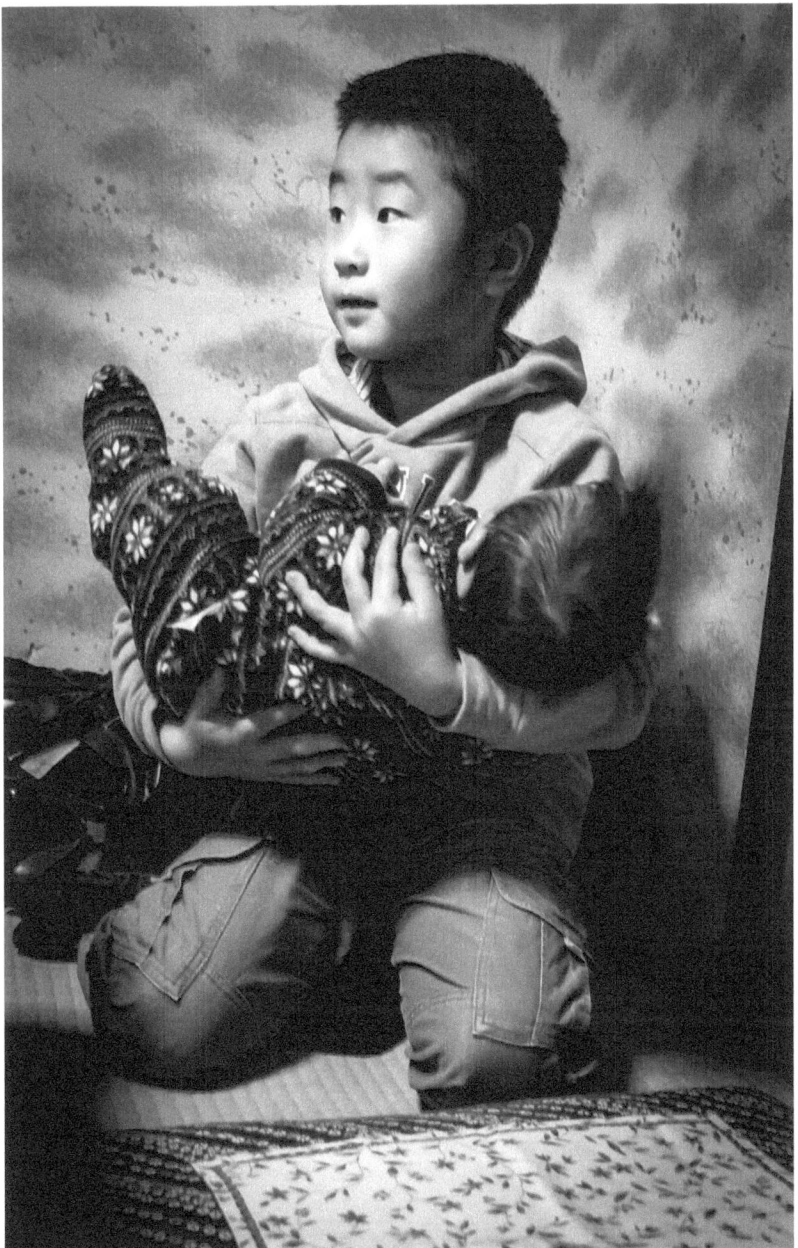

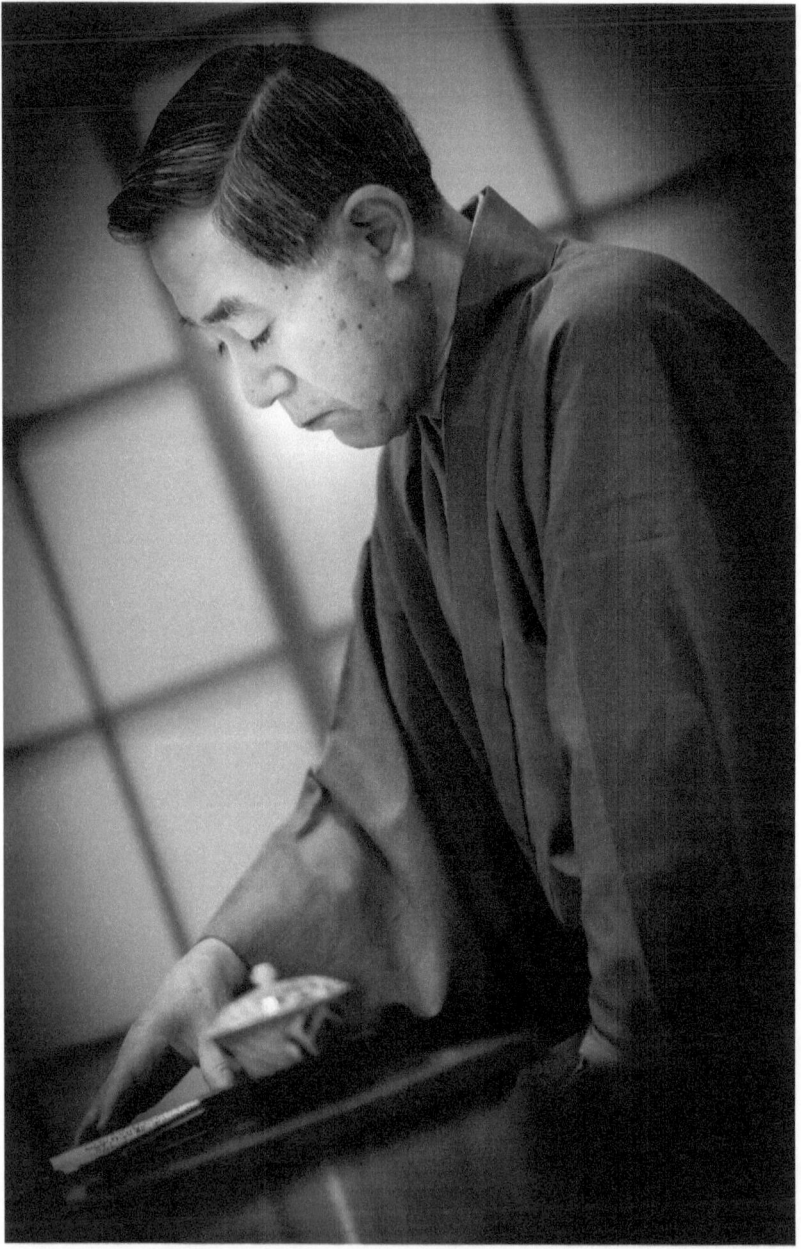

REHEARSAL
AT MY MASTER'S MASTER'S
HOUSE

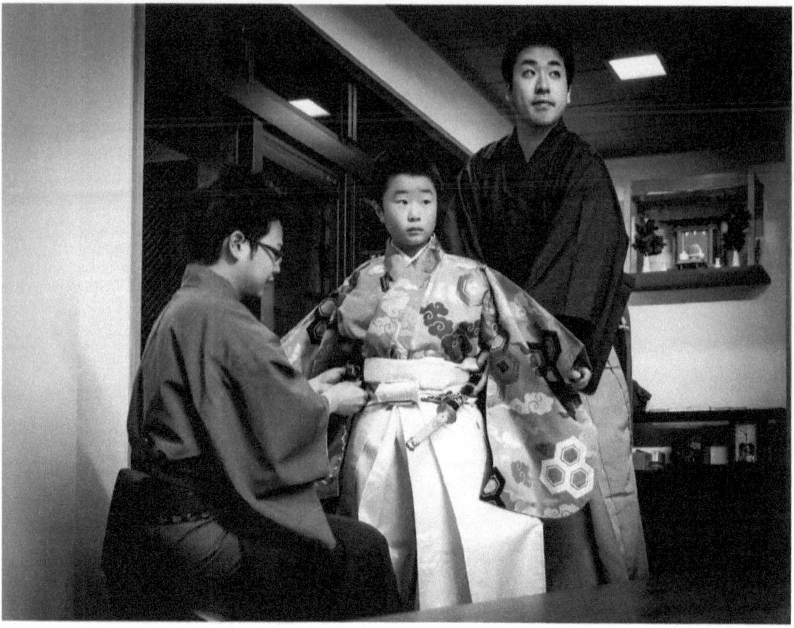

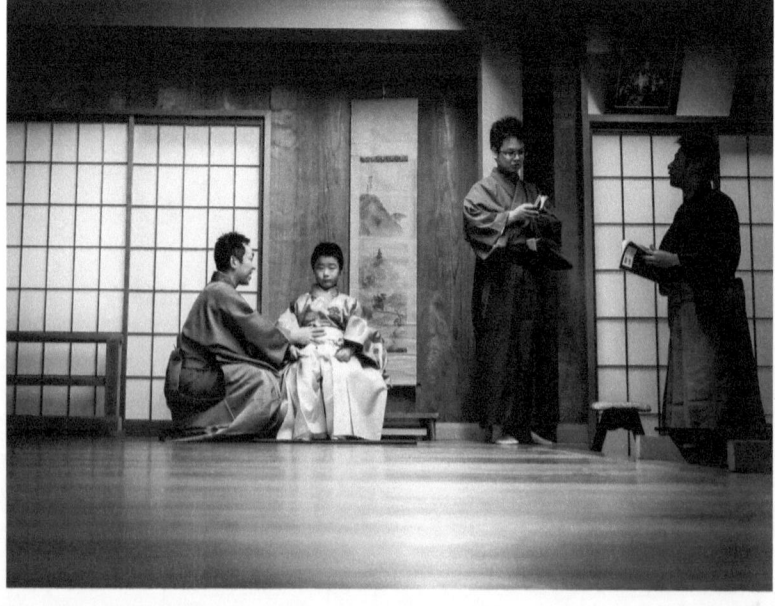

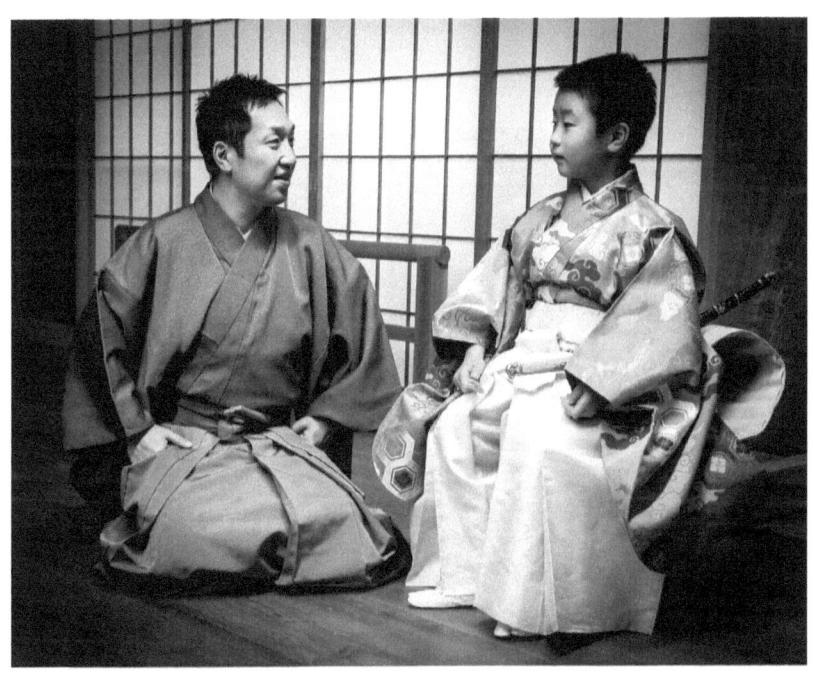

Today, we rehearse at the home of my master's master with the students who live there. My kimono is beautiful in orange and green. I look like a little prince.

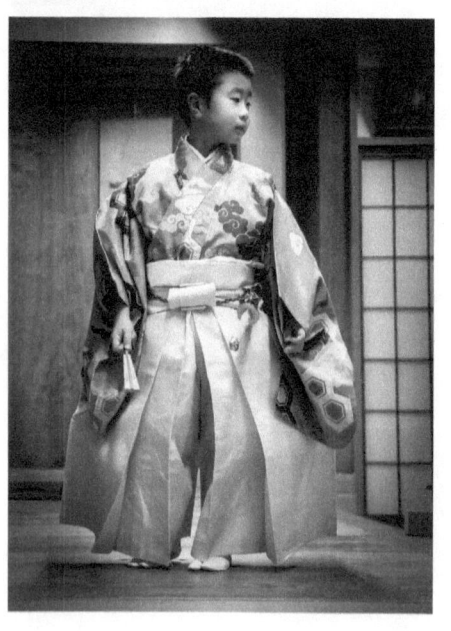

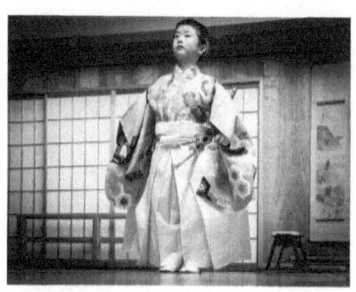

My master asks me to recite my part with my strongest voice. I open my mouth wide.

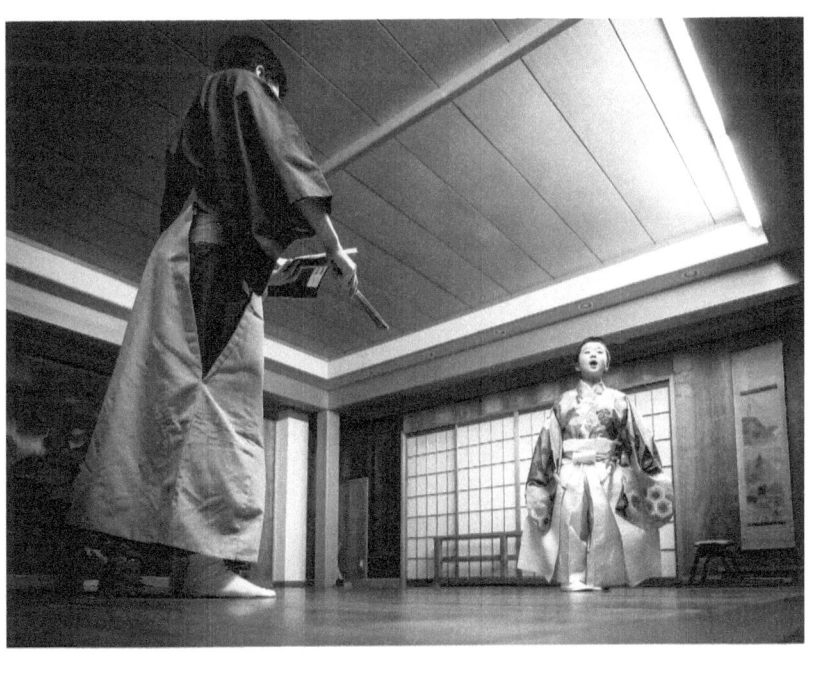

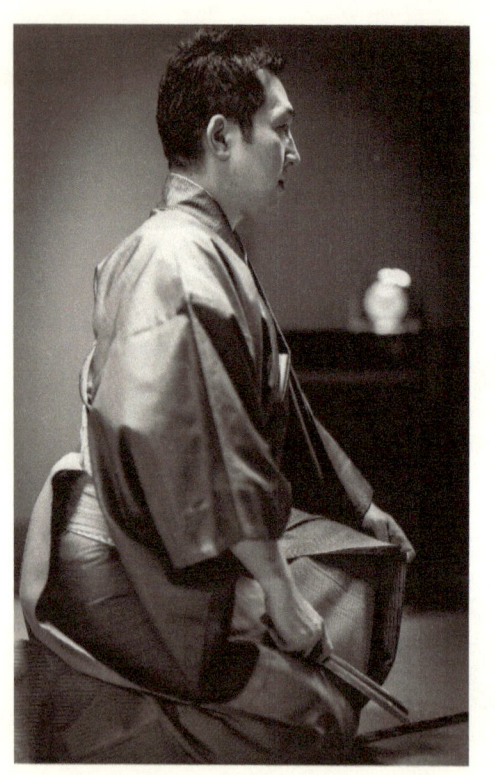

Today, my master is very focused. He is no longer a teacher.

He makes me think of the athletes in the finals at the Olympics.

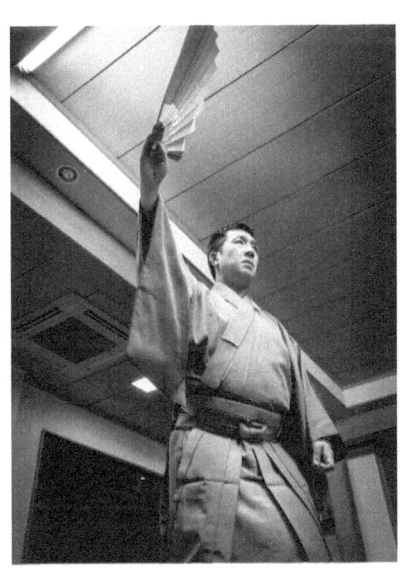 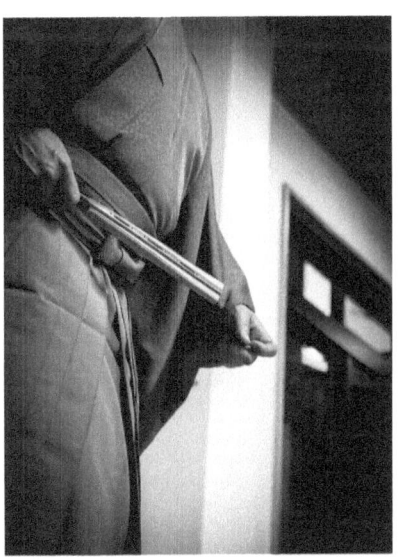

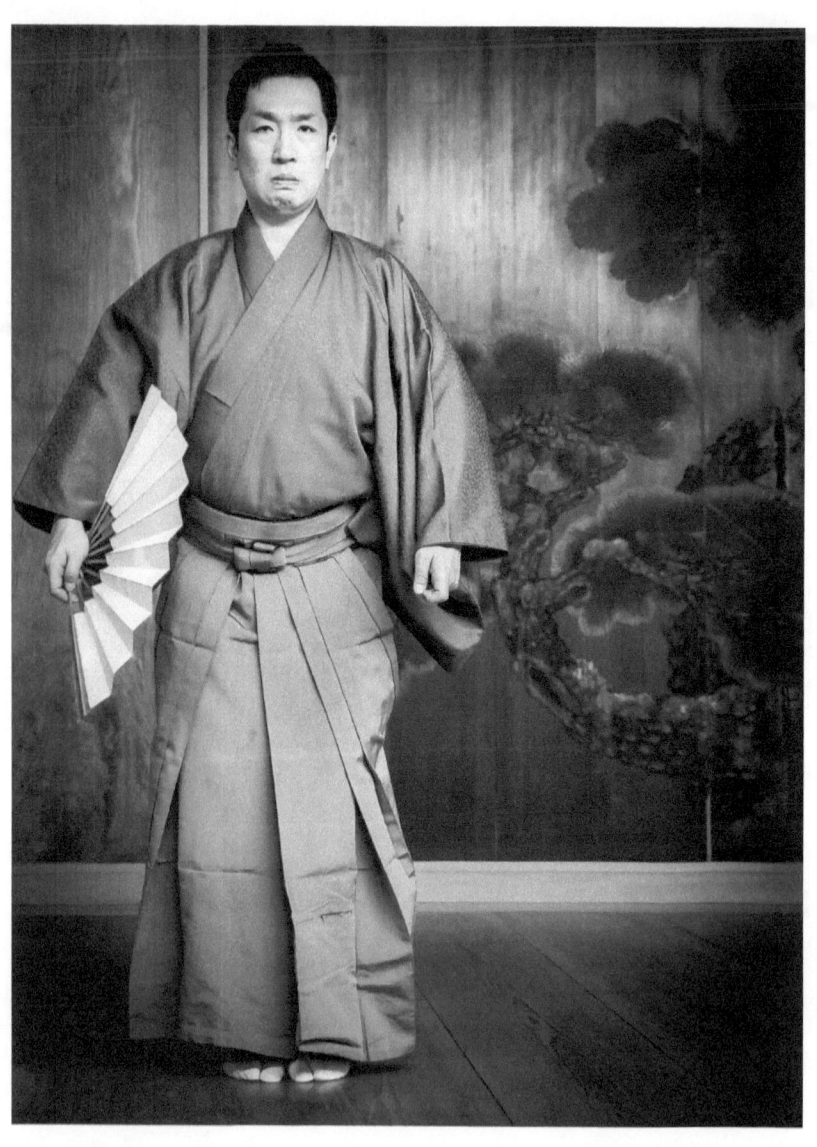

Even his face is different.

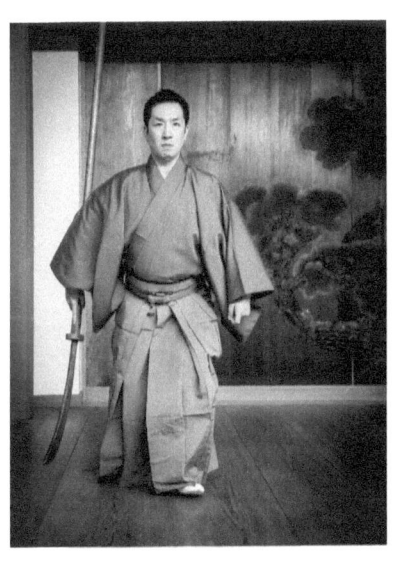 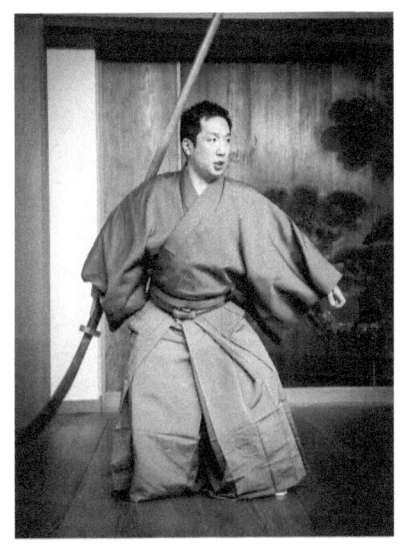

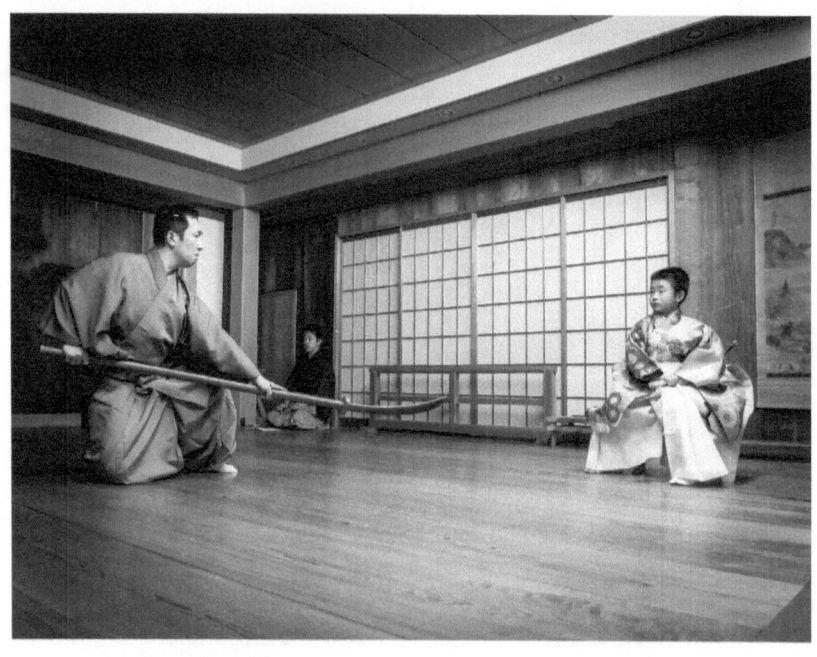

On my master's master's wide stage, my fight against
the monster and his spear looks like a movie.

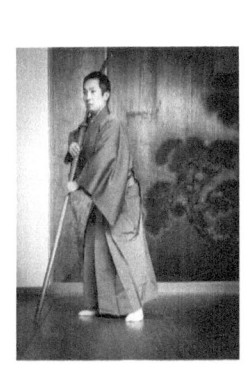
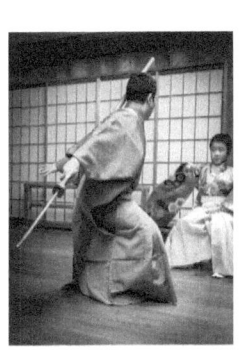
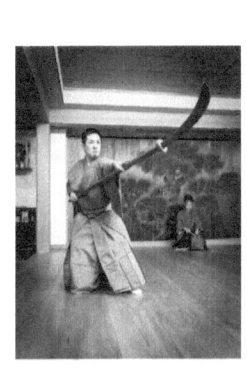

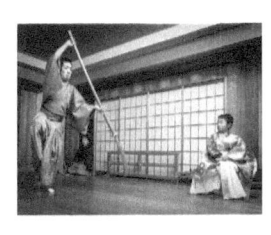
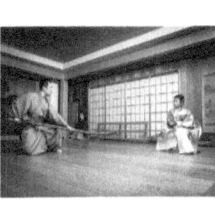
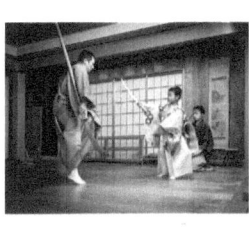

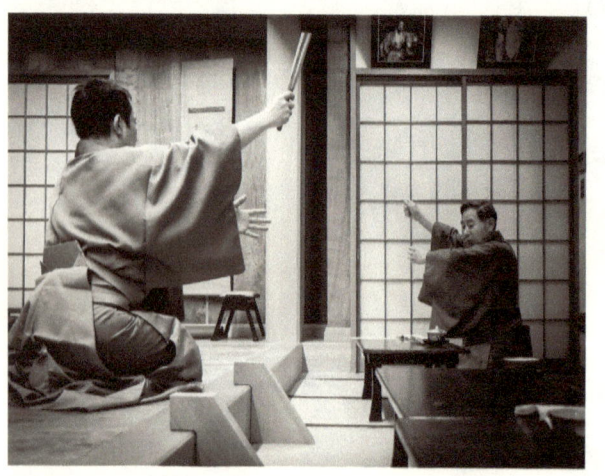

After the rehearsal, my master's master, who had been silent, took a moment and then made a list of everything that had to be improved.

I was surprised by all the small details he had seen.

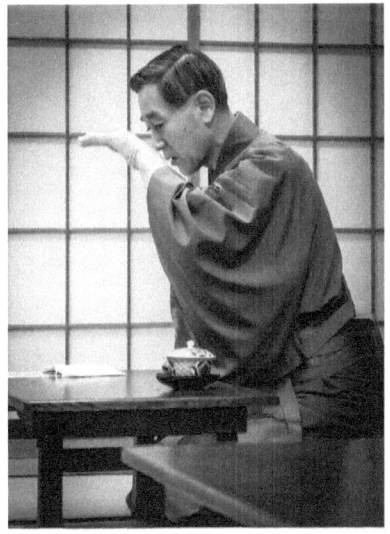

He went on stage to show what couldn't be said in words.

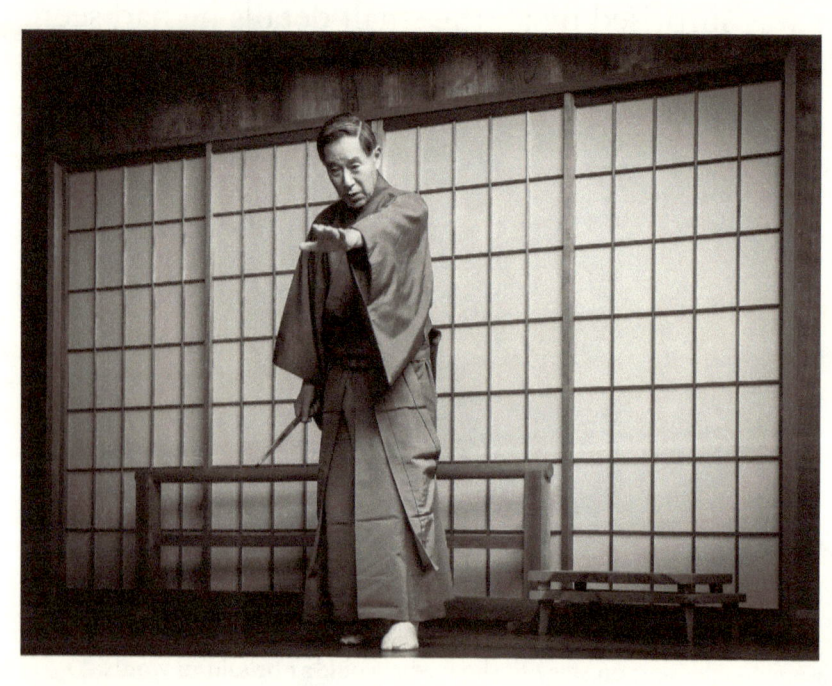

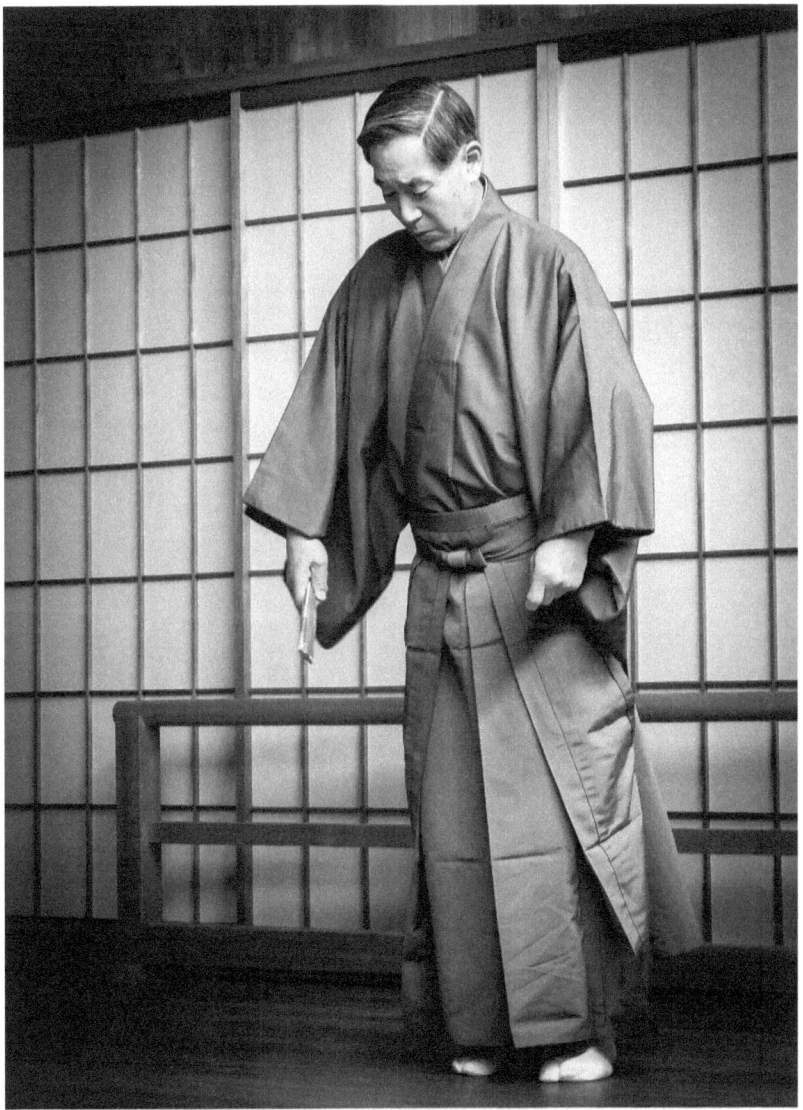

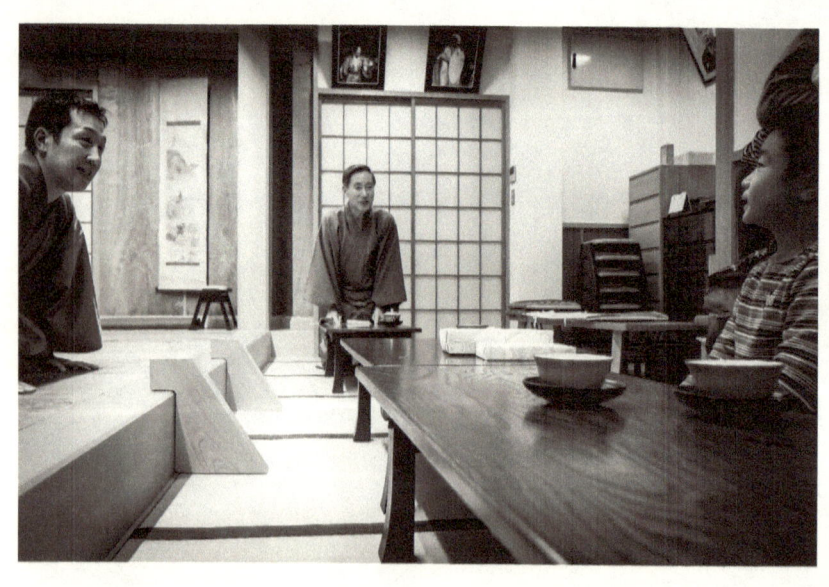

At the beginning of the session, my master's master looked very stern and barely said anything.

But at the end of the rehearsal, his voice changed. He spoke to me gently while drinking green tea brought by his students.

I wonder if he remembered the first time he played Yoshitsune when he was my age. I wonder if he liked to be the strongest samurai or if he was sad because he didn't have a choice since his dad was a noh master and he had to do the same.

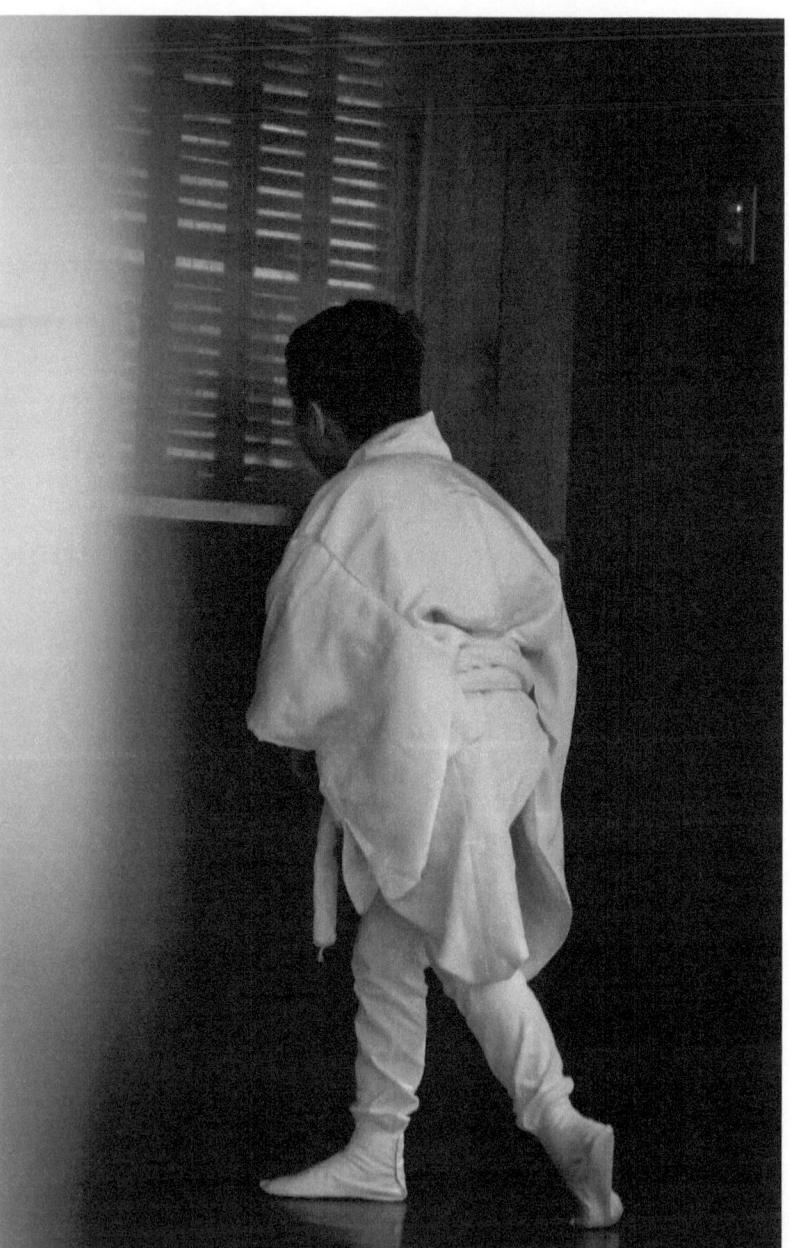

THE DAY
OF THE PERFORMANCE
Behind the stage

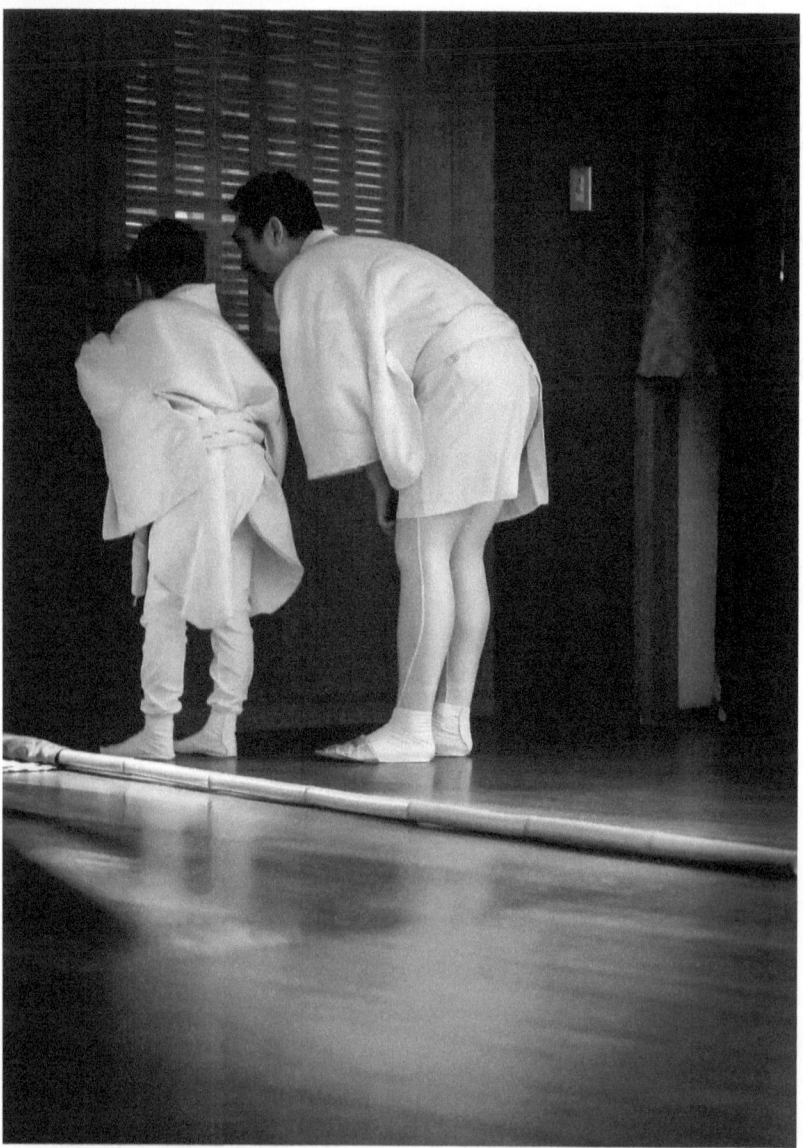

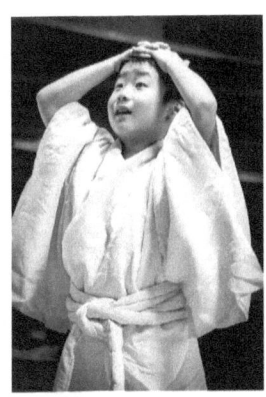

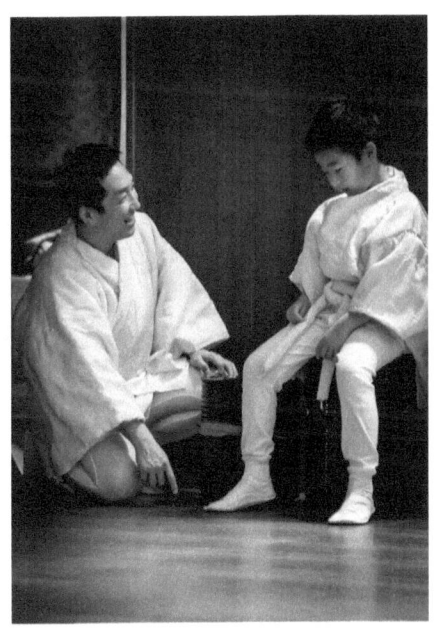

On Sunday, it's finally the performance! I thought about it all night. The first play just finished. Ours is the second one. I can see the audience. There are only adults and old people. My master looks relaxed.

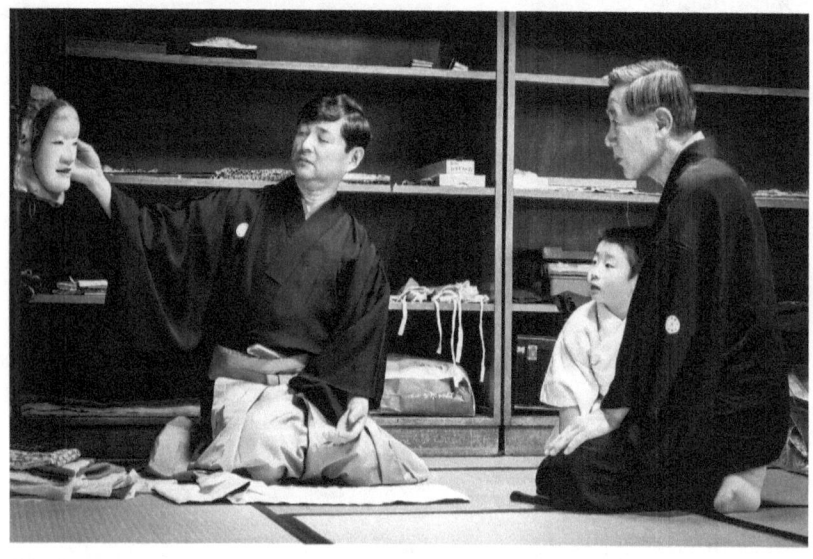

My master's master played the main role in the first play.
Another master asked for his permission to look at his mask.

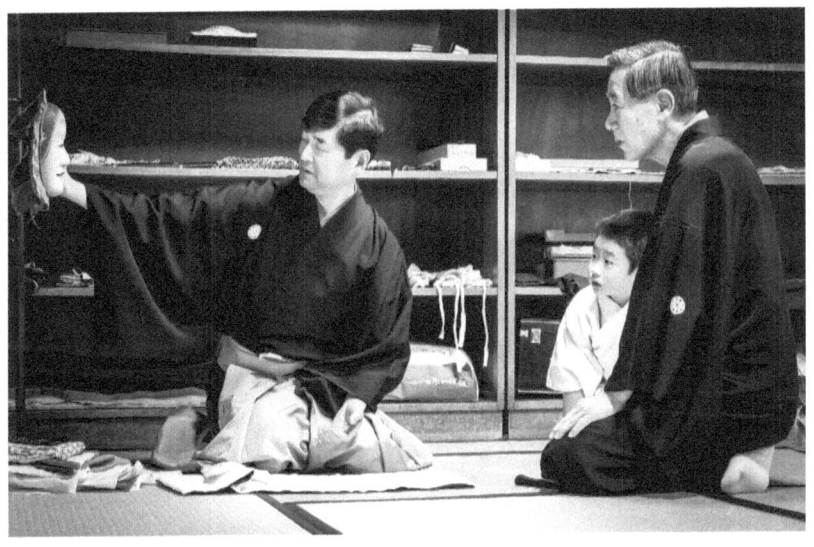

A noh mask is magical: if you move it a little bit to the right or to the left or up or down, it changes. It becomes sad or it smiles.

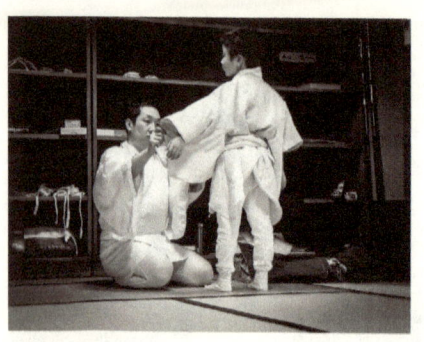

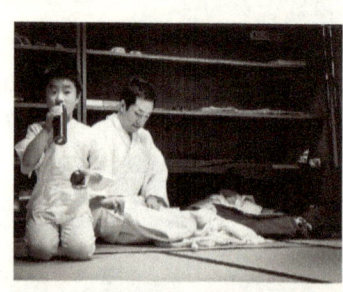

What impresses me back-
stage is the calm.

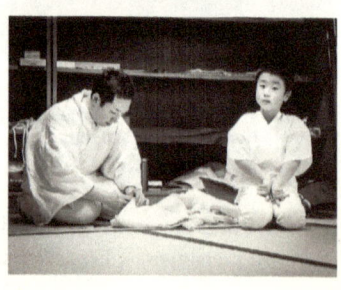

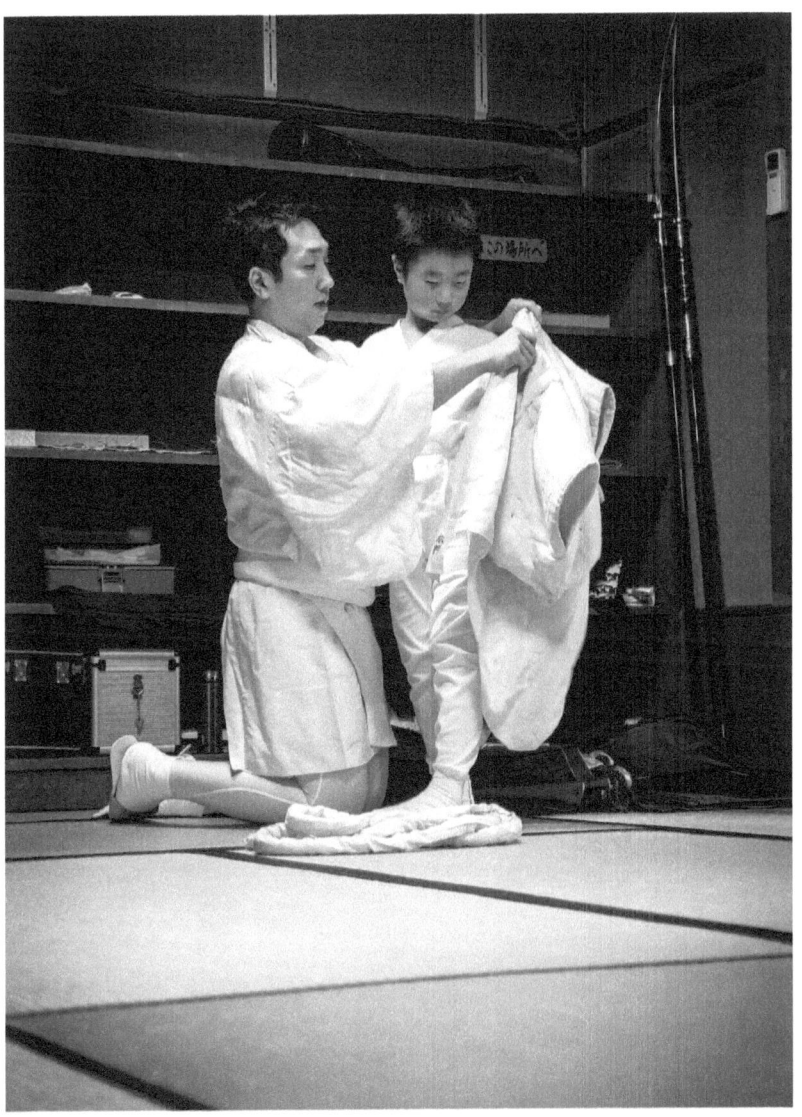

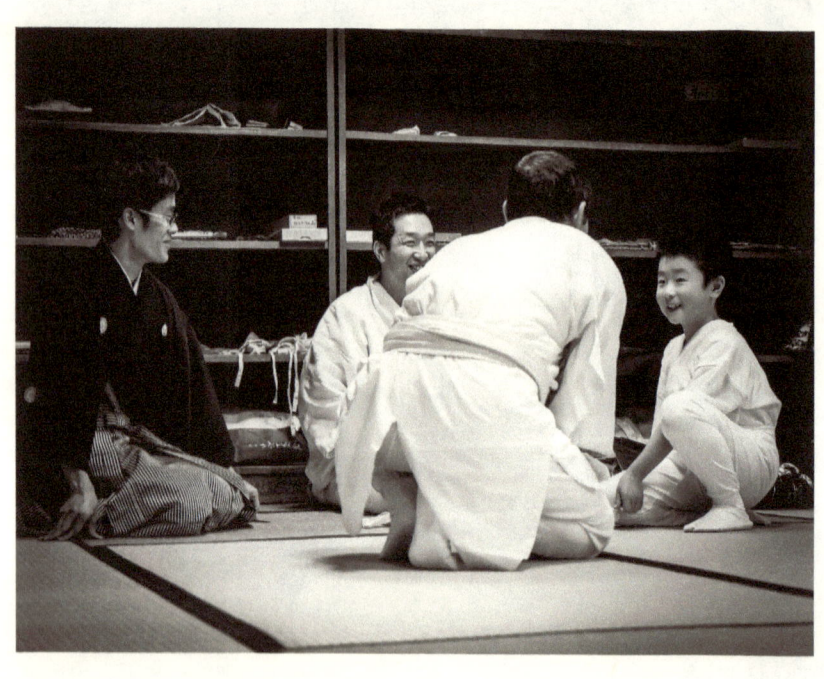

The kyogen master came to ask me how I'm feeling.

Kyogen masters can make everyone laugh in just a few seconds. If I do not become a noh master, I will be a kyogen master.

Everything was calm and then all of a sudden, all the masters came to help us get dressed.

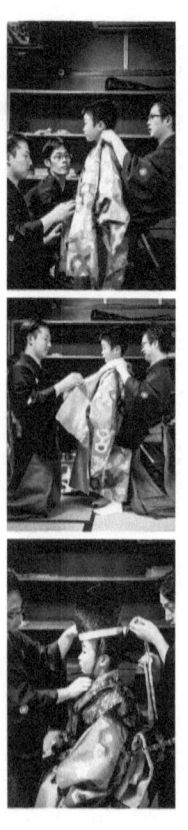
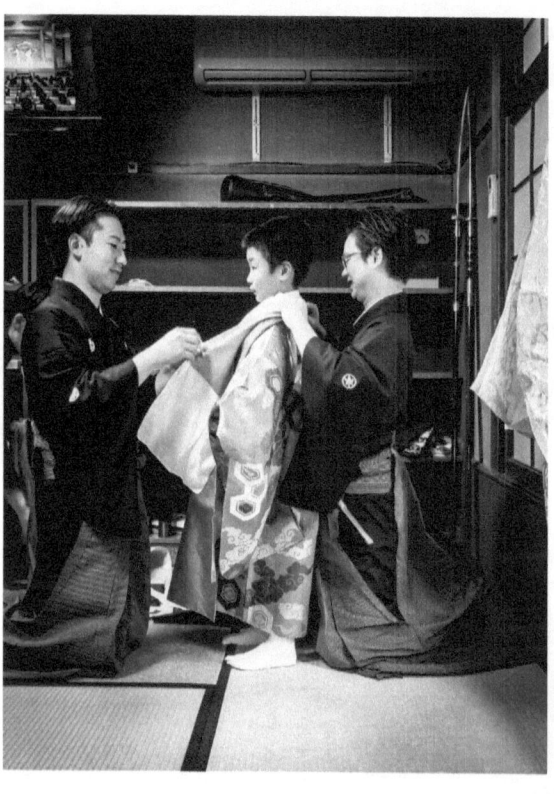

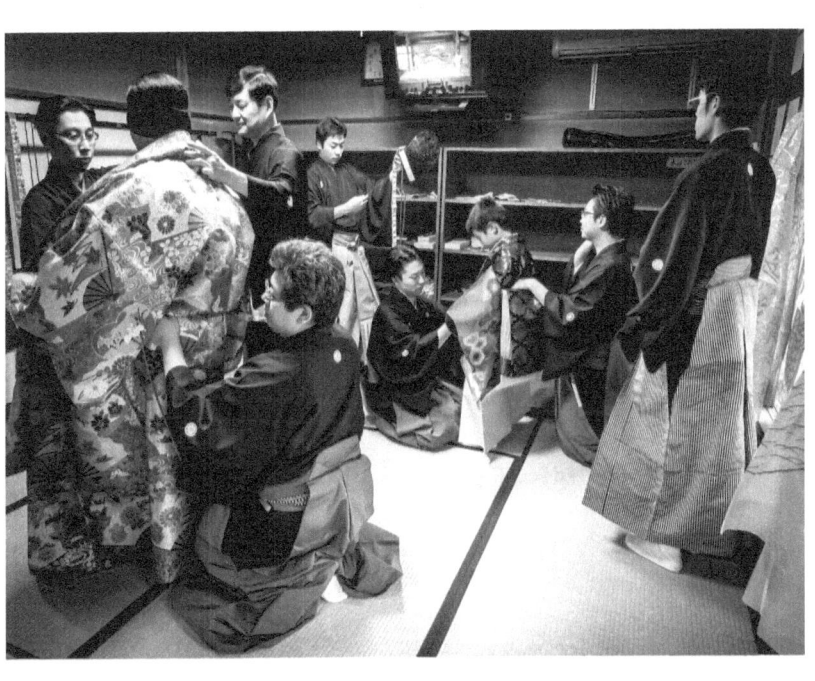

In a few seconds, the room was full. But everyone was relaxed and smiling. Focused but happy, like they were preparing for a party.

It's a little surprising to see adults, dads, being able to prepare costumes like a bridal kimono. Tying them with silk thread sewn directly with needles so they stay in place during the dance. Combing long-haired wigs. Before, I thought it would be assistants and moms who would take care of the costumes.

But here, all the masters help each other get dressed, making complicated knots and perfect folds with woven kimonos that are so precious that they're only worn for the performance. The knots are really important! They shouldn't be too tight, but if they're not tight enough, the kimono could come undone during the battle!

The more I see what the masters know how to do, the more I understand how amazing they are. I wish the audience could see how great they are behind the scenes.

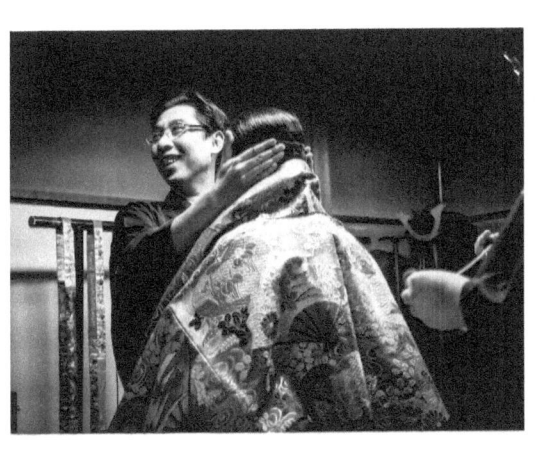
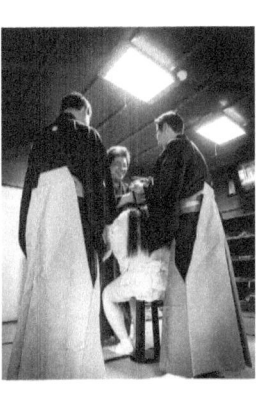

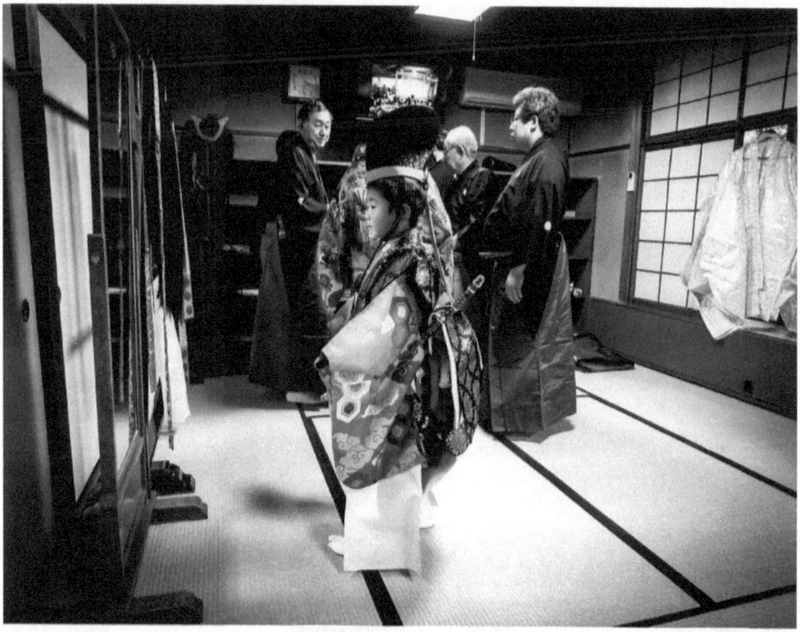

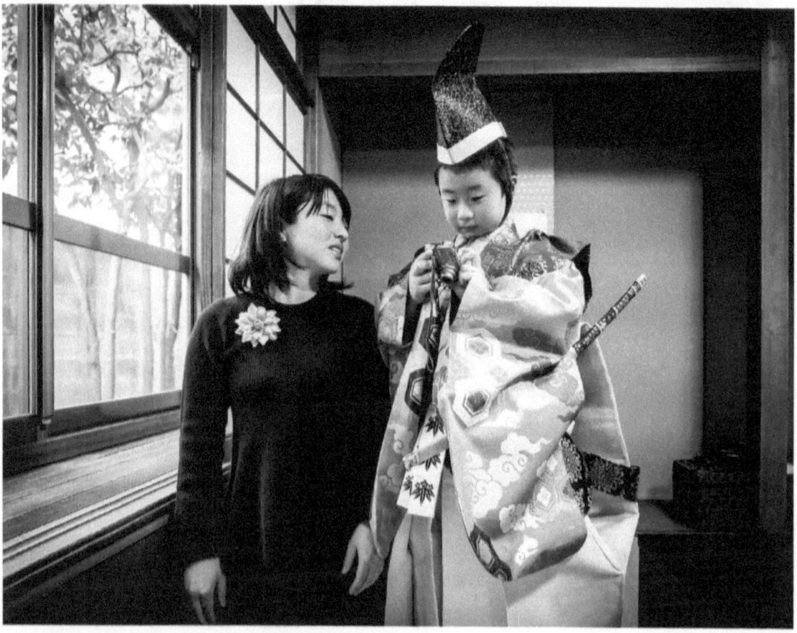

That's it. I'm ready. I really like
my costume. I like the colors,
designs, and golden threads.
And I love my hat.

I wait for my master's prepara-
tion to finish. I walk down the
hallway behind the stage. And
then into the mirror room.
The one where you have to
wear white socks to enter.

I feel ready.

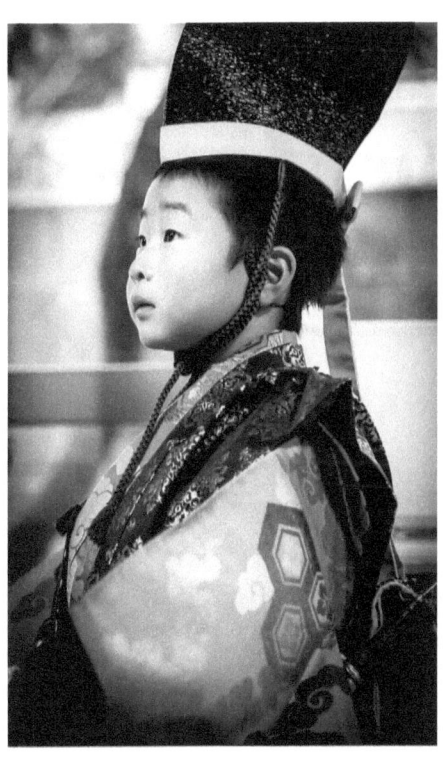

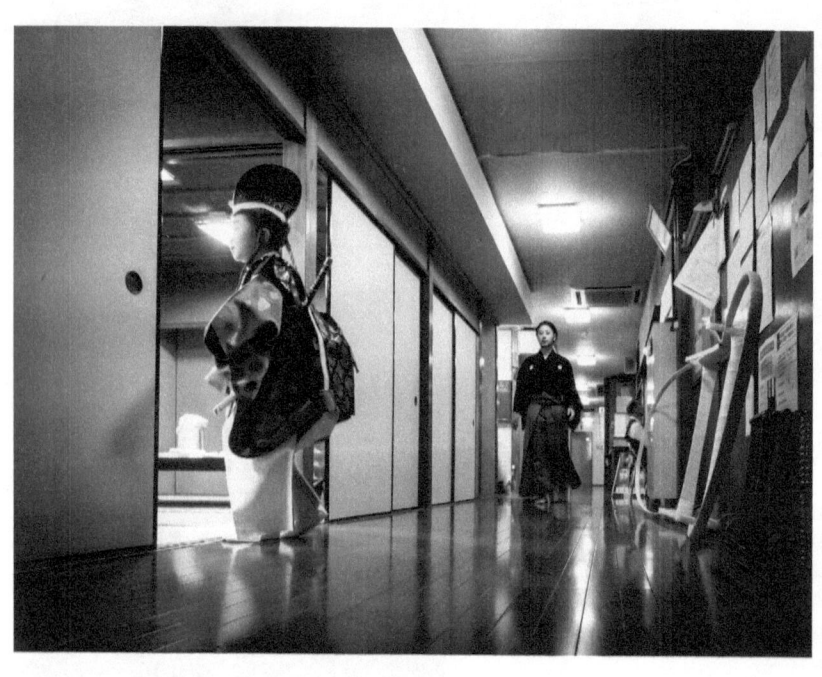

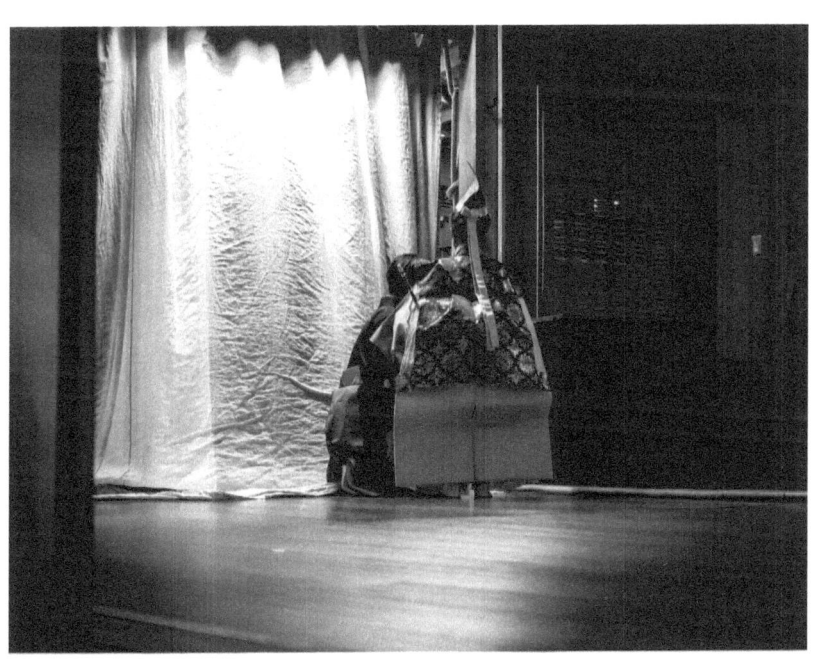

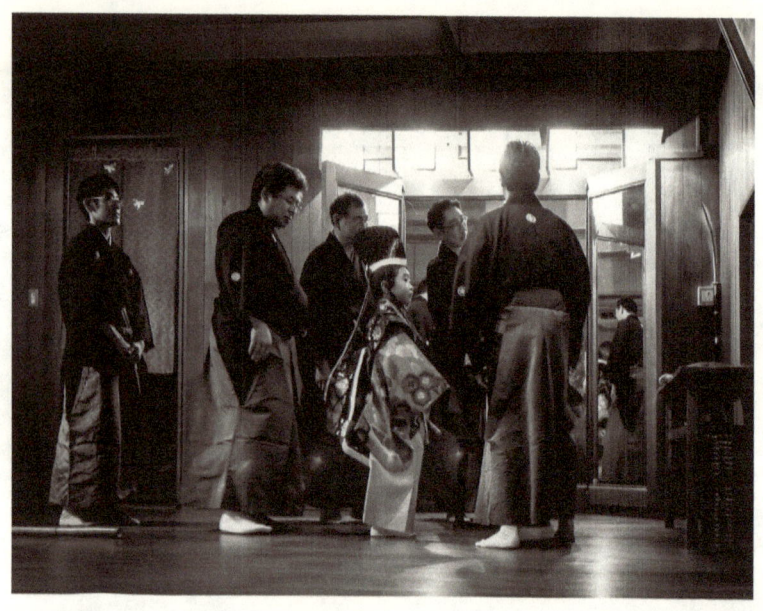

In the mirror room, the mood has changed. Everyone speaks in a whisper. Everyone is totally focused. We check my kimono one last time and the musicians settle down for the oshirabe.

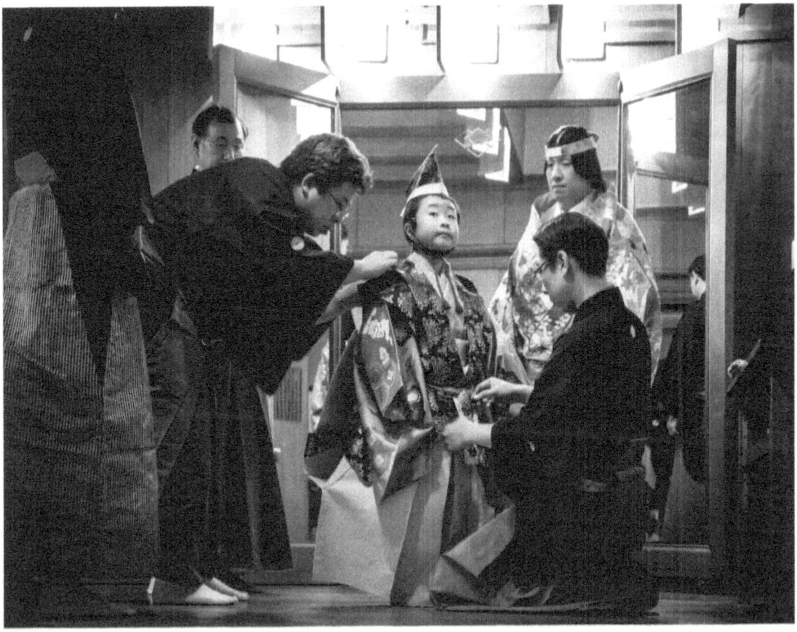

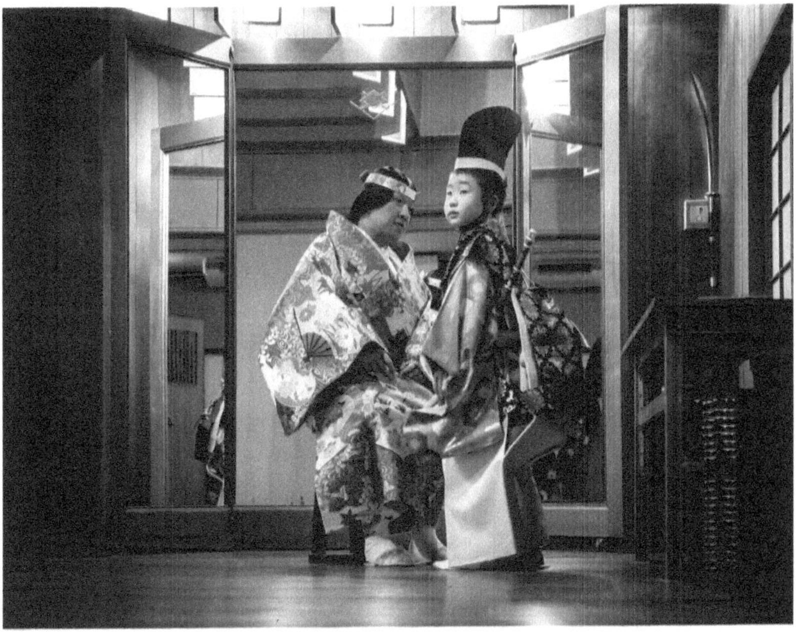

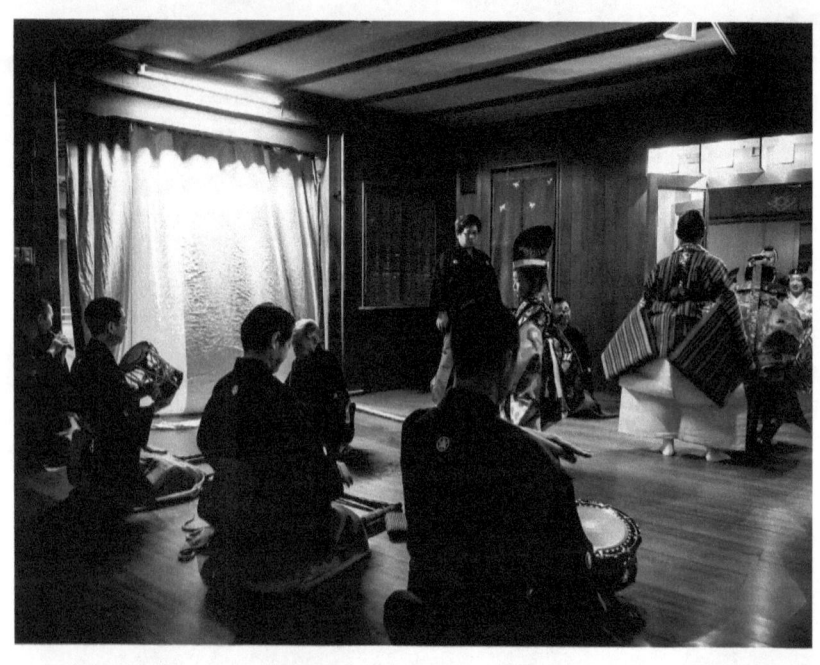

I like the sound of the oshirabe. The air stays in me.

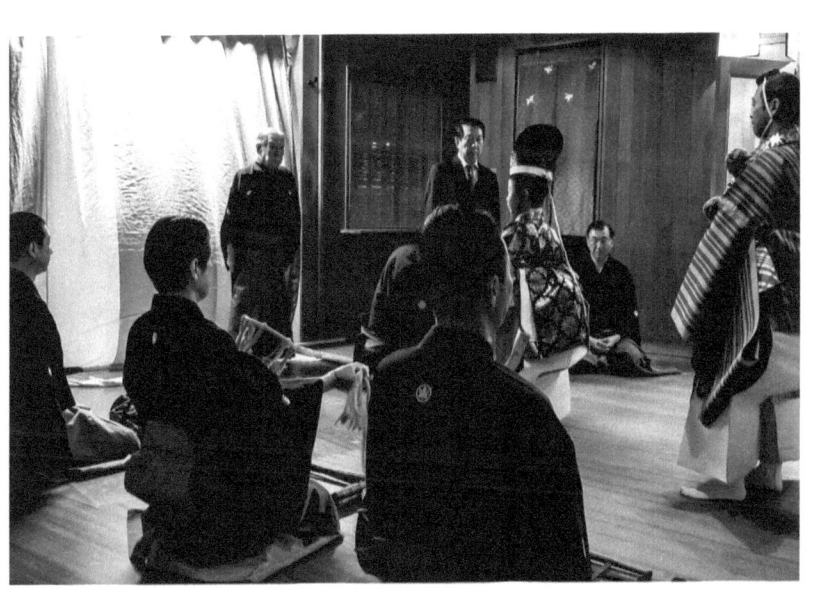

I'm ready to enter Yoshitsune.

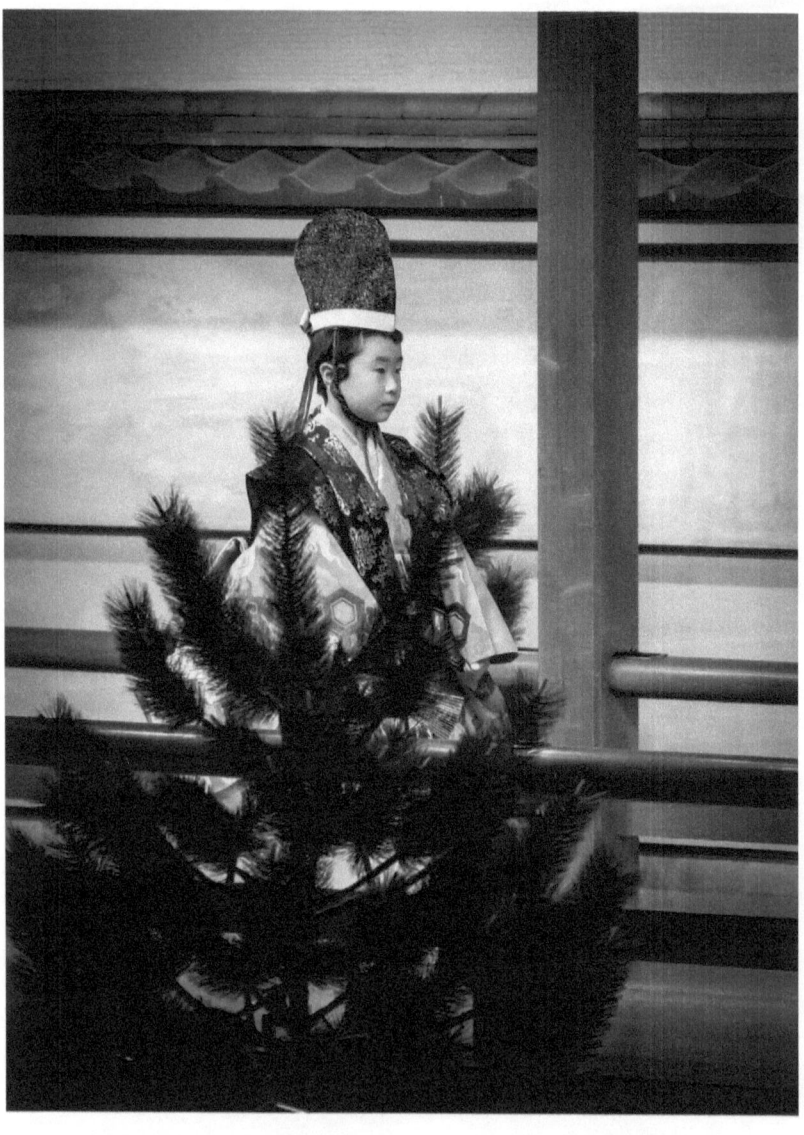

THE DAY
OF THE PERFORMANCE
On stage

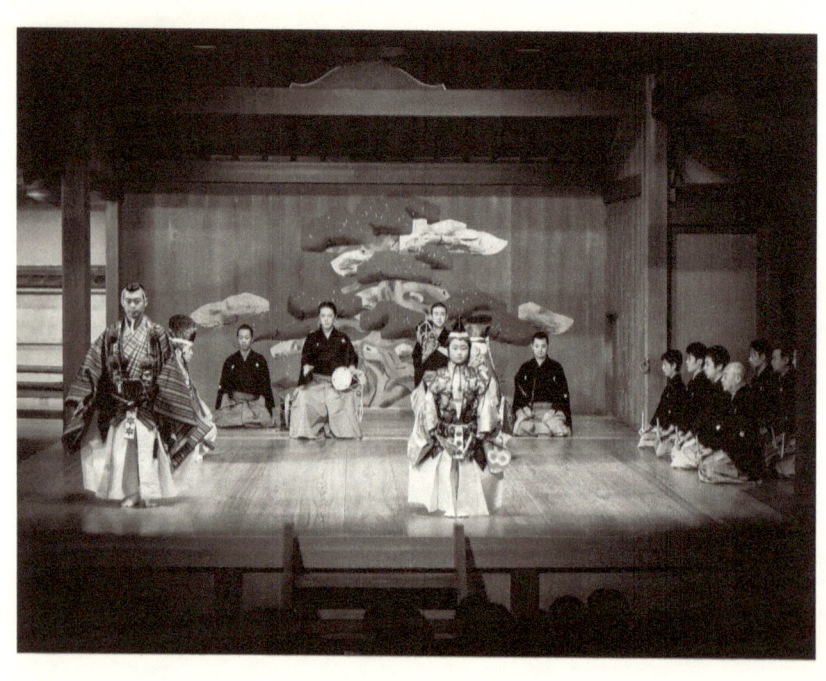

It's not like the only rehearsal we had three days ago.

The room is not lit, but we can still see the whole audience. It looks like a big ceremony. Like at the temples. Or the ones during the festivals.

It's not like school. It feels like a family.

It's as if everyone is part of the same group. As if everyone, we on stage, and the audience in the room, were making one.

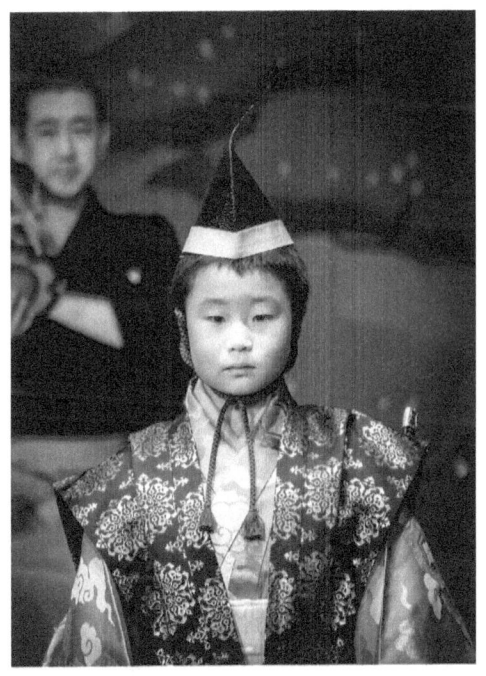

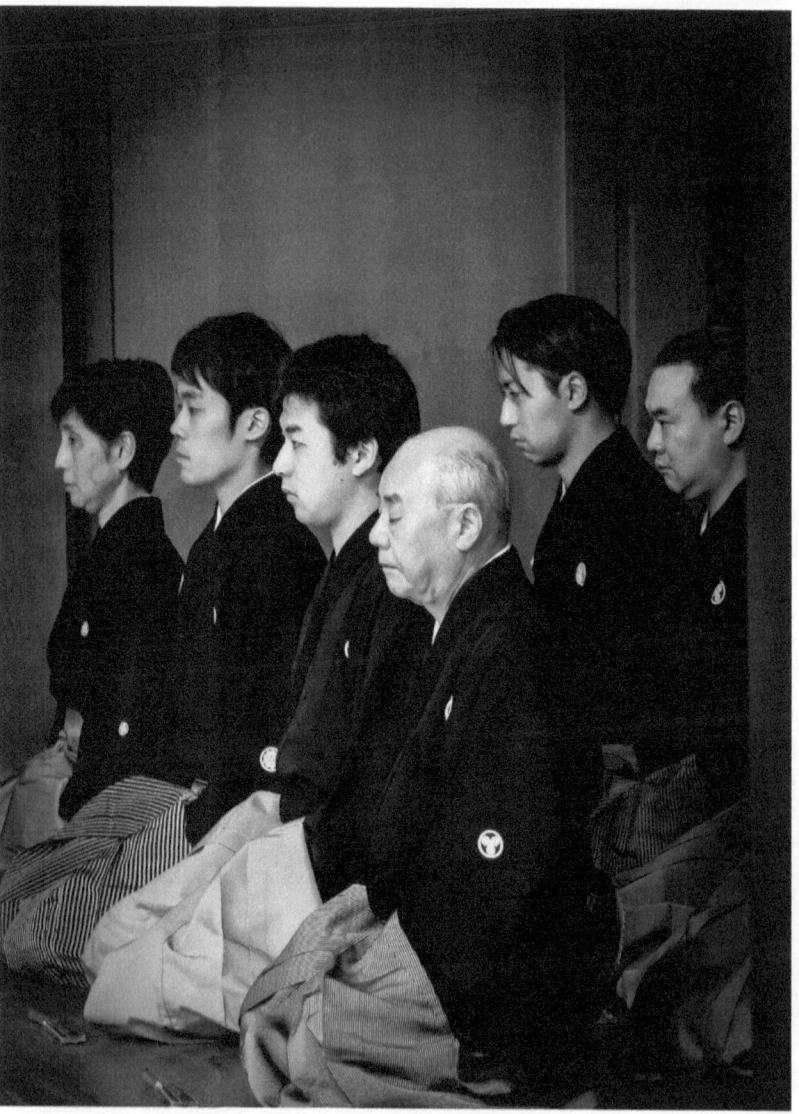

I like the choir that sings with a deep voice.

In the choir, there are old sensei, a lady sensei (I thought there were only men but it's not the case anymore), very young sensei and sensei who are my master's age.

There is a master in the middle of the second row that all the others listen to and follow. He is the choir leader and he carefully synchronizes with the drum.

I asked my dad what our family kamon is, to imagine how my black ceremony kimono will look one day. A Kuromonzuki is more beautiful than a tuxedo.

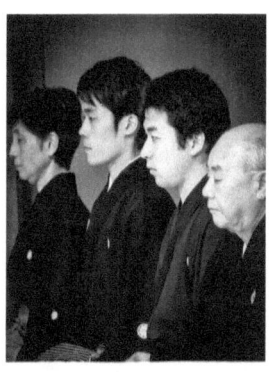

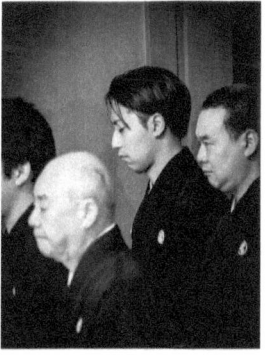

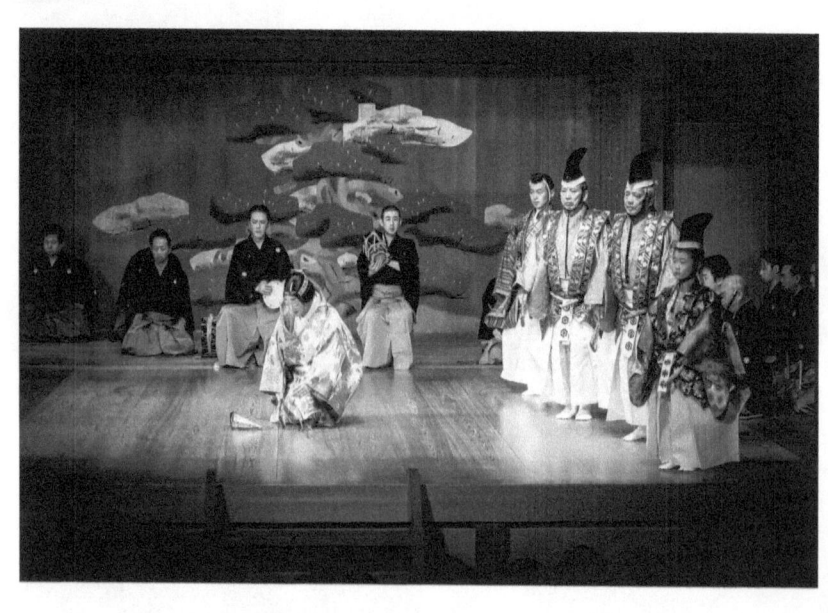

My name is Yoshitsune. I'm 26 years old. I am the greatest warrior of all time. My big brother is the ruler of the country.

I am the greatest because I won the war against the enemies, the Taira family, who wanted to become the rulers and replace us. In the final battle fought at sea, they all drowned.

But after my victory, a jealous general on our side convinced my brother that I wanted to take his place. Since then, he wants to kill me. So I'm running away. It's totally unfair.

I am accompanied by two guards and my most faithful guardian: the warrior-monk Benkei (he is played by a waki with a small round hat on his forehead). He is super strong. And super clever. Without him, I would have died many times. So I always listen to him.

And so far, my girlfriend has also managed to accompany us. She is very beautiful and we love each other. Her name is Shizuka.

I don't know how all the masters can sit in seiza for so long.

If you look carefully, sometimes they move just a little, without showing on their faces how much they're suffering. I don't know if it's normal to suffer to create art. They're all really beautiful on stage. But still!

When I become a noh master, I might do as the clever ones do: I will put a small wooden plank in my pants to put my buttocks a little higher so I feel less pain in my knees.

Today, I'm lucky. A master has prepared a round stool for me. It helps to play a great prince!

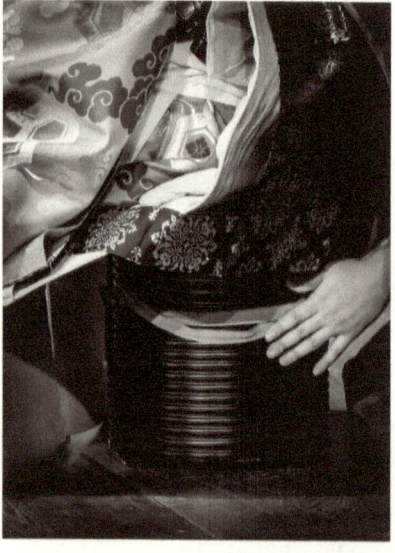

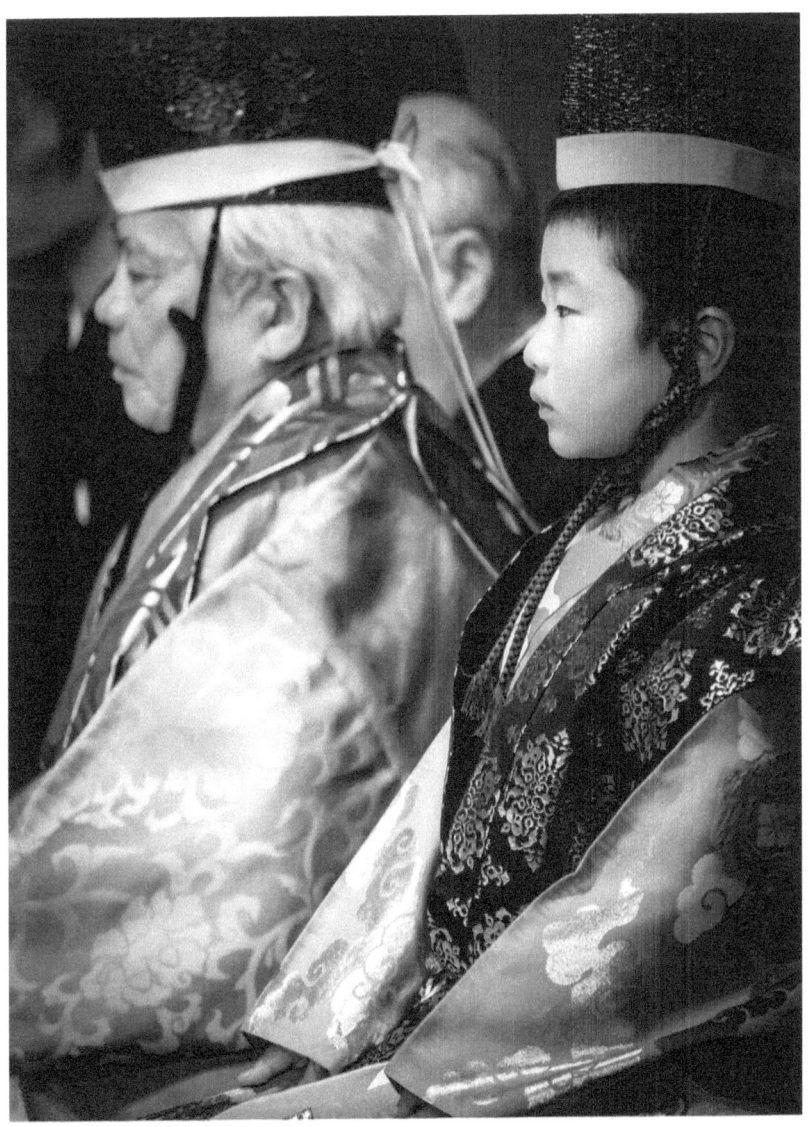

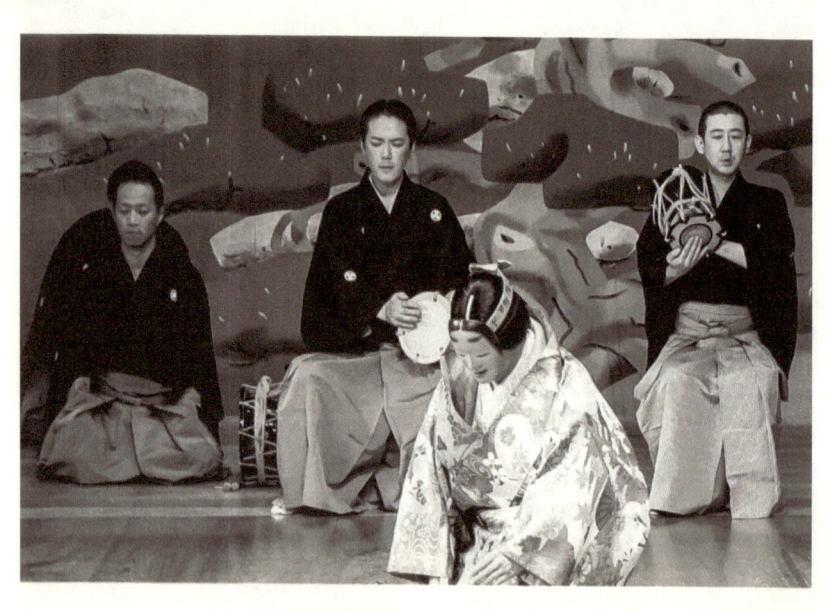

Another way to have a chair is to be one of the drum players: either the hip or shoulder drum.

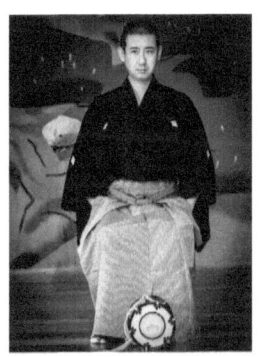

They are the only ones who are allowed to sit on a small foldable chair with a cushion! They even have helpers to set them in place.

I asked, but no one knows why.
Maybe there was an important master in the past who had sensitive buttocks or knees.

If I were the flute or the taiko, I'd be jealous.

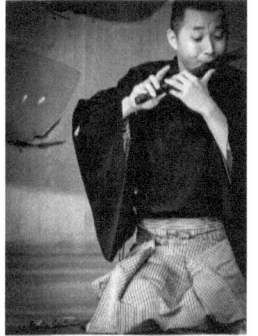

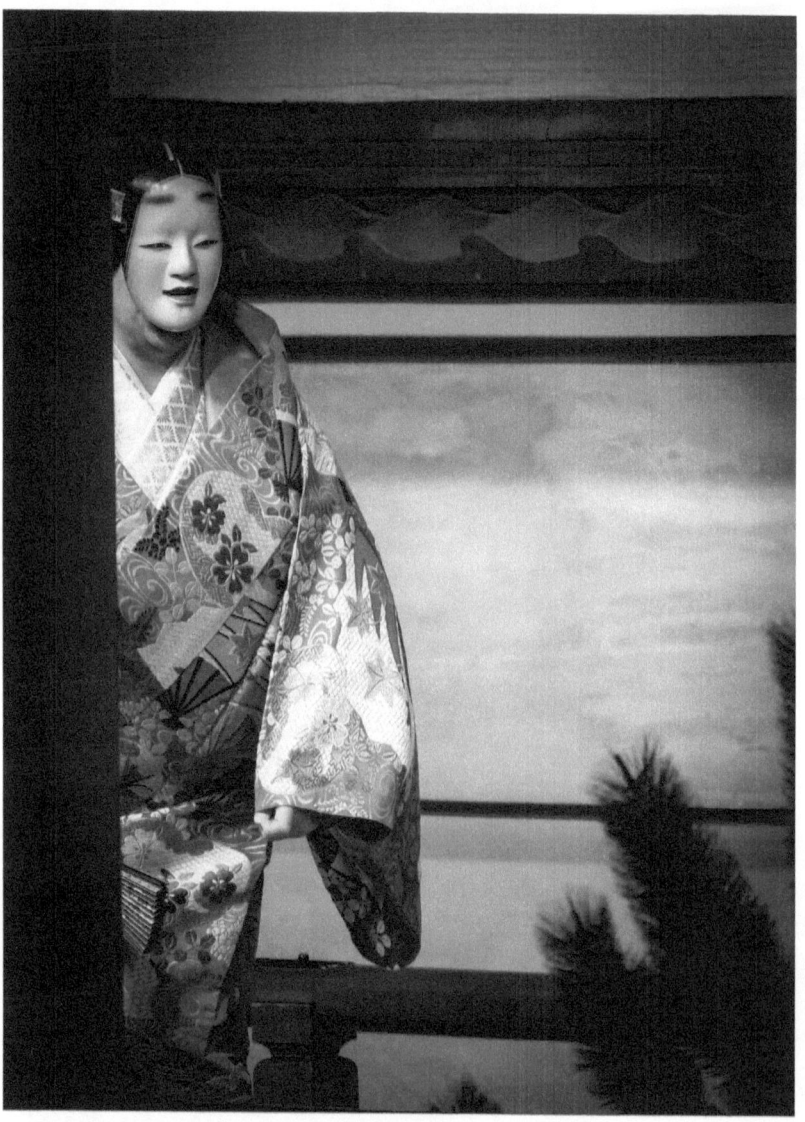

Tomorrow morning, we have to take a boat to go to the West by sea. It's dangerous and if we have to take care of Shizuka, we risk being caught and killed.

So Benkei wisely tells me that it's better for her to return to the capital to wait for a while.

At first, she did not want to believe him. She wanted me to tell her directly.

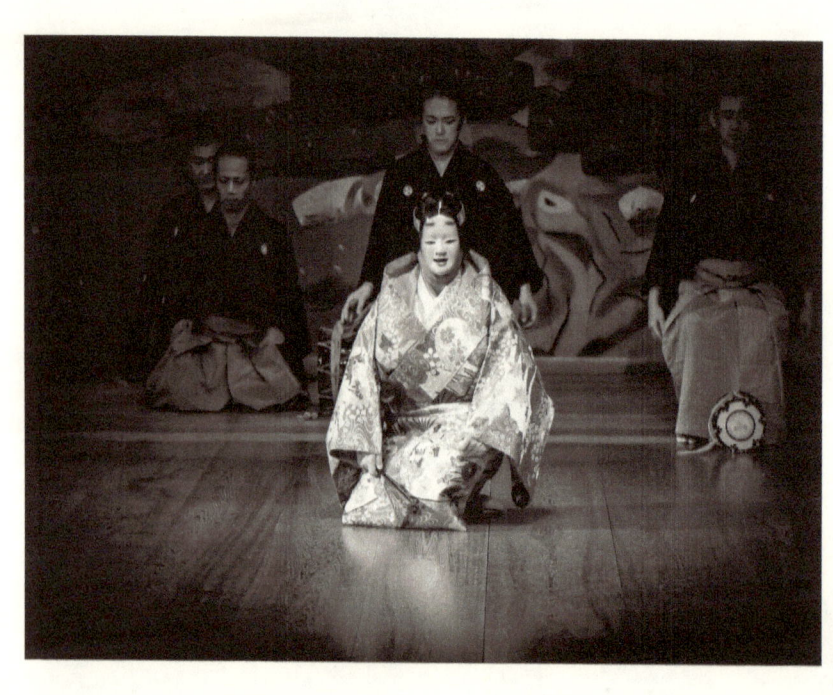

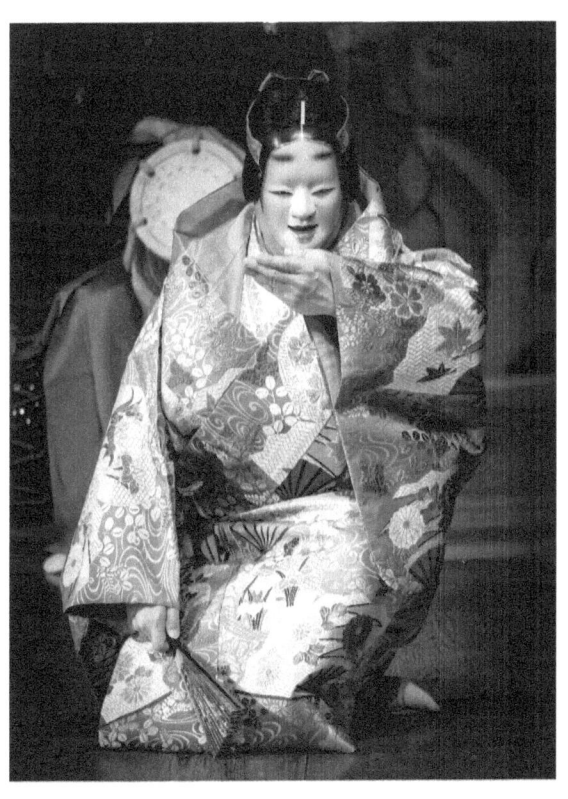

So I told her. It was not easy but I told her and she started crying.

We drank wine mixed with flowers to comfort her, but she kept crying and crying. So we asked her to sing a poem for us.

I gave her one of my hats and she danced to an old Chinese song and then she hid her face behind her fan because she was suffering so much.

At school, when someone is crying, I don't like it. I wonder if adults feel the same.

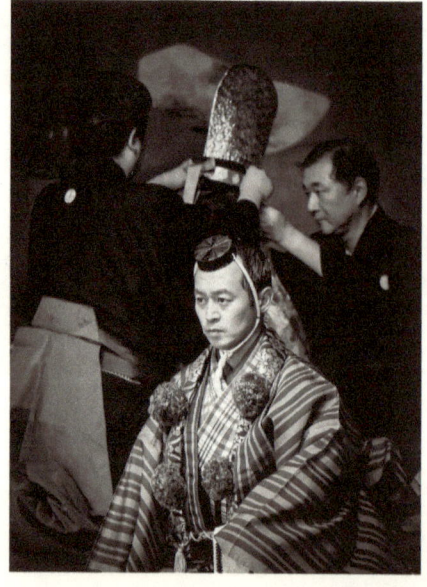

Noh can be weird: I don't understand why a boy plays the role of an adult.

And why aren't the roles of girls played by girls? They would be better, for sure. Because of the master's deep voice, it's not really believable when he plays a crying woman in love.

And then there's something else: the way we speak in old Japanese in the play. No one understands anything. It's worse than how my grandmother talks, the one who lives in the countryside. Sometimes, with my friends, we play around and talk like gangsters or like in old movies. But in noh, even my mom told me that she doesn't understand. The master had to explain every word of the old language to me. And I still didn't understand everything. So I memorized the sounds like a song in English.

I keep this to myself. I wonder if adults tell each other that they don't understand.

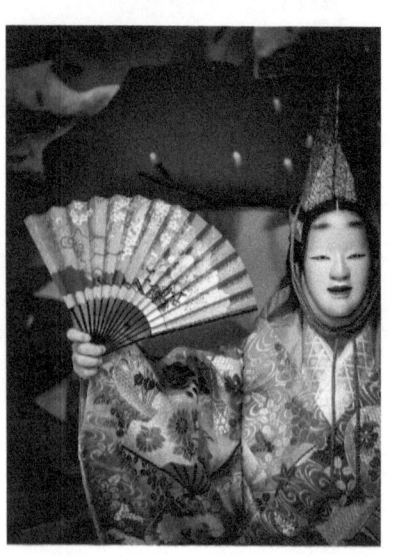 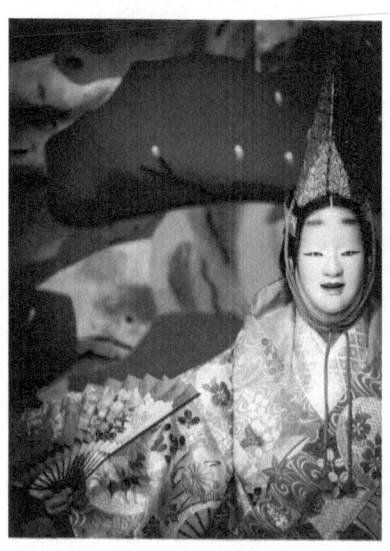

At the end, Shizuka dances and recites another poem that prays to Kannon for me to come back safely so that we can finally be together.

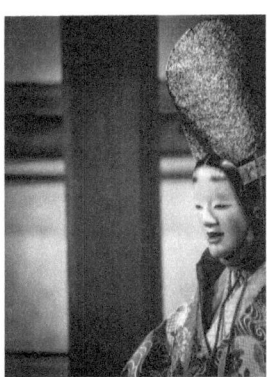

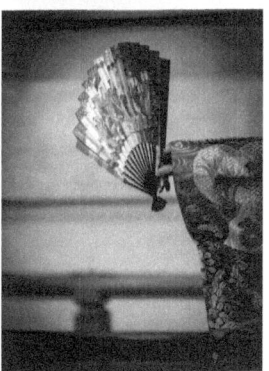

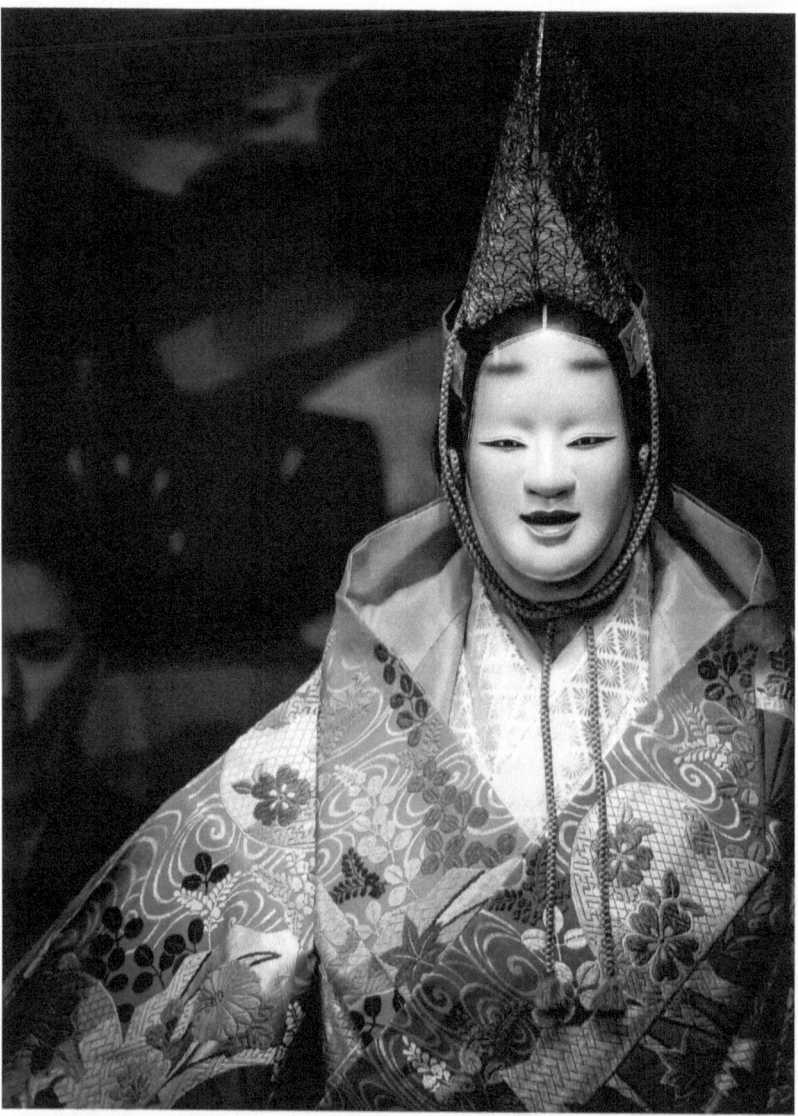

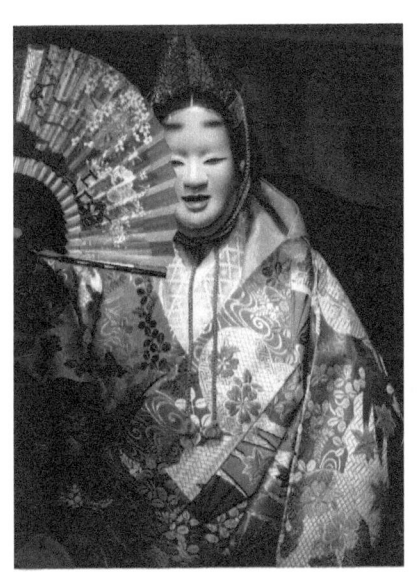 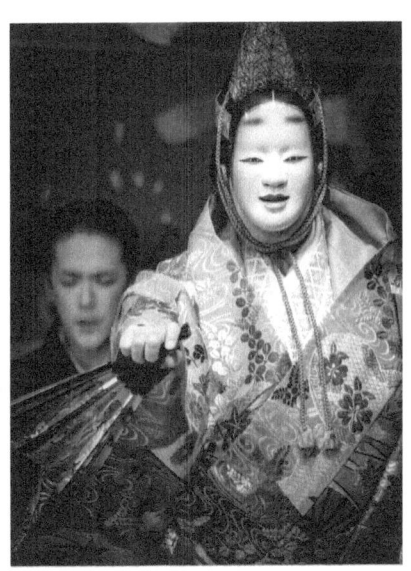

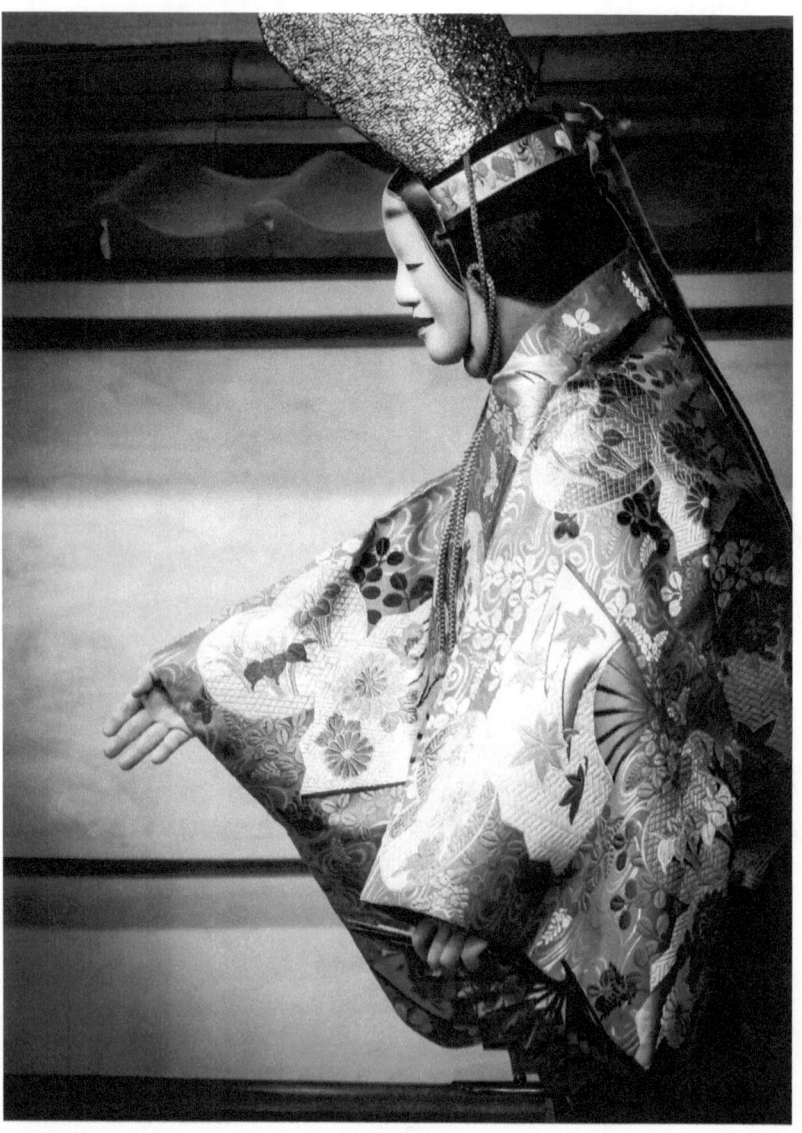

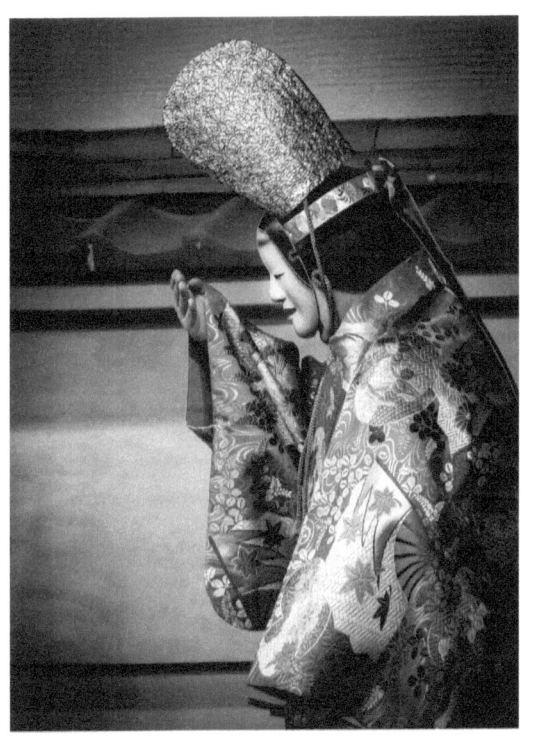

And then, she cries, she cries more, and then she leaves.

It's a very strange story. During half of the play, we only talk about Shizuka with her super beautiful kimono and then just like that, she disappears and my master becomes someone else totally unrelated. It's like there are two stories in one with the same actor playing both main roles. It's good that he wears a wooden mask so no one can recognize him. Maybe they can't afford two actors?

Mom told me that it was more complicated because in noh, shite, the actors who wear the masks and dance like my master, they are the ones who have to organize everything and pay everyone:

- the flutist who plays music which doesn't really sound like music, but who doesn't make anything up when he plays: like for everyone else, everything is written and has been memorized by heart.
- the drum players who make funny cries like wolves.

- the choir that sings so loud and so deep that they sound at least double their number.
- the waki who do not wear masks and who come on stage first and sit for a super long time on one knee.
- the kyogen who make jokes and who always tell a long story between the two parts of the play which no one listens to, but which gives the shite time to change costumes.
- the koken, the helpers who are there to adjust the costumes on stage, to whisper the lines if someone forgets, or to replace the shite if, by some accident, he can't continue. I would like to have a koken for my tests at school.

And then the shite has to also rent the costumes, book the stage and pay for the photos and the video. At least there are no stage sets in noh!

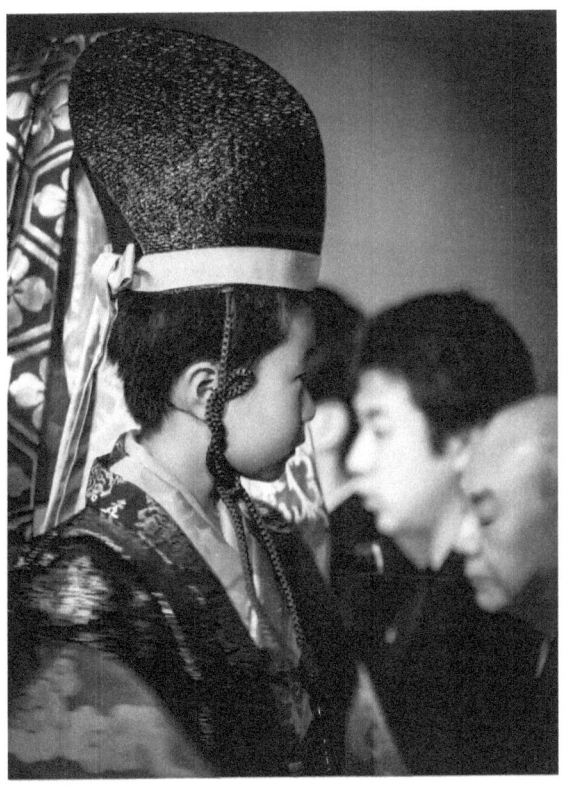

A play costs so much that often, instead of making money for all their work, the shite use their own savings and they can't do as much as they would like. They must really love noh to sacrifice themselves like this!

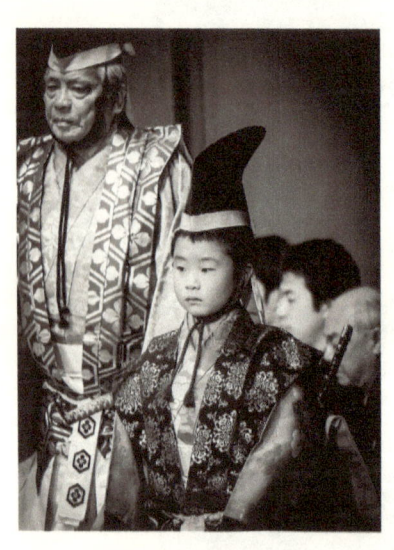
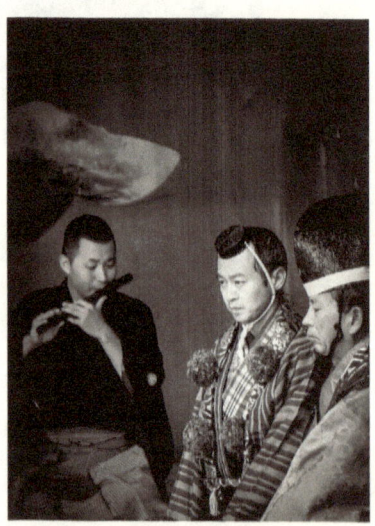

While everyone is ready to leave, I send one of my soldiers to tell Benkei that it would be better to postpone our departure because there could be a storm today.

In fact, Yoshitsune does not want to leave Shizuka. Dad says it's because he wants to kiss her. Mom replied no, it's because he loves her and wants to stay with her as long as possible.

I agree with Benkei. During the final battle in the boats against the Taira, there was also a storm and Yoshitsune won, so the real reason is not the weather. I don't like that the brave super warrior hesitates like this.

That's why I'm happy when he finally decides to get on the boat.

To rehearse in our living room, I made a boat like the one in the play with two chairs and two brooms. My mom was not happy because she doesn't like it when I play with the brooms.

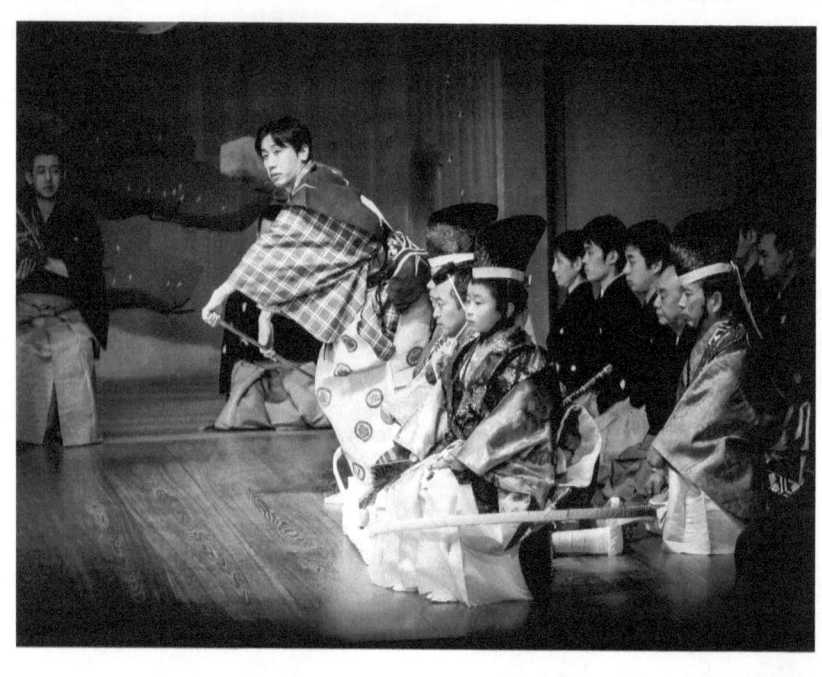

The kyogen enters. Unlike everyone else, kyogen wear yellow socks. I like the kimonos of the kyogen: their colors and their designs. Except the ones that have a big turnip in the back. I don't like turnips.

Here, the kyogen plays the man who will row the boat from the the rear. He tells Benkei that he saw Shizuka crying and that he had shed some tears, too. Benkei says that he did, too and that what's happening is really unfair. I wonder if this first part was written for girls because I think it's like the TV shows that my mom watches where everyone cries. It's good there's the second part with the action and the combat!

The kyogen reminds me of our neighbor who's a taxi driver and who always talks loudly about the weather and about how he wants to be rich. It's the same here: the kyogen tells Benkei that we are lucky that the weather is good, that everything will be fine, and that when Yoshitsune returns to the capital some day, it would be really nice if he could appoint him chief of the boats for the West, and that we should not forget him. This boat driver is not very polite.

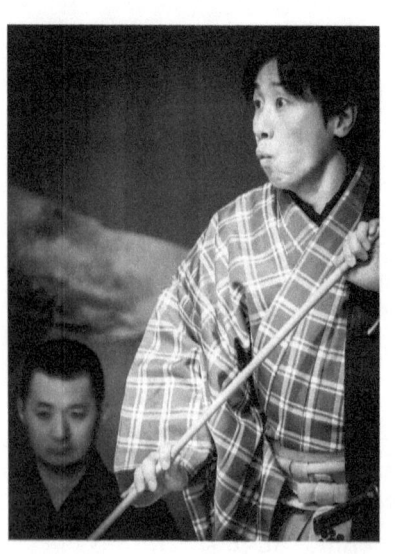
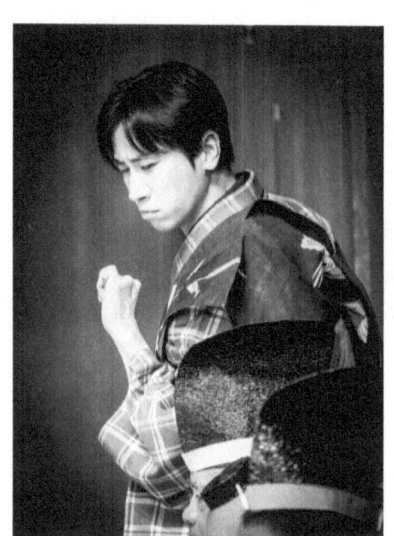

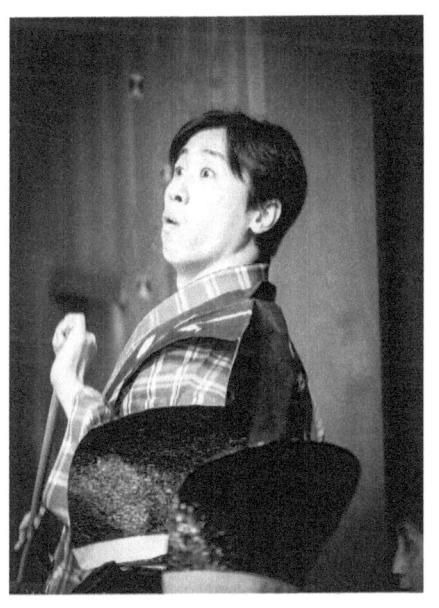

And then I suddenly change my opinion about him because the sea changes. The winds become really strong and the waves really high. The kyogen starts saying that he is afraid and that we should pray. And we can see that he is doing his best to guide our little boat and it must be very difficult with the big waves. The kyogen is really good at creating the feeling of the storm just by moving with his body.
I couldn't do it at home as well as he does it.

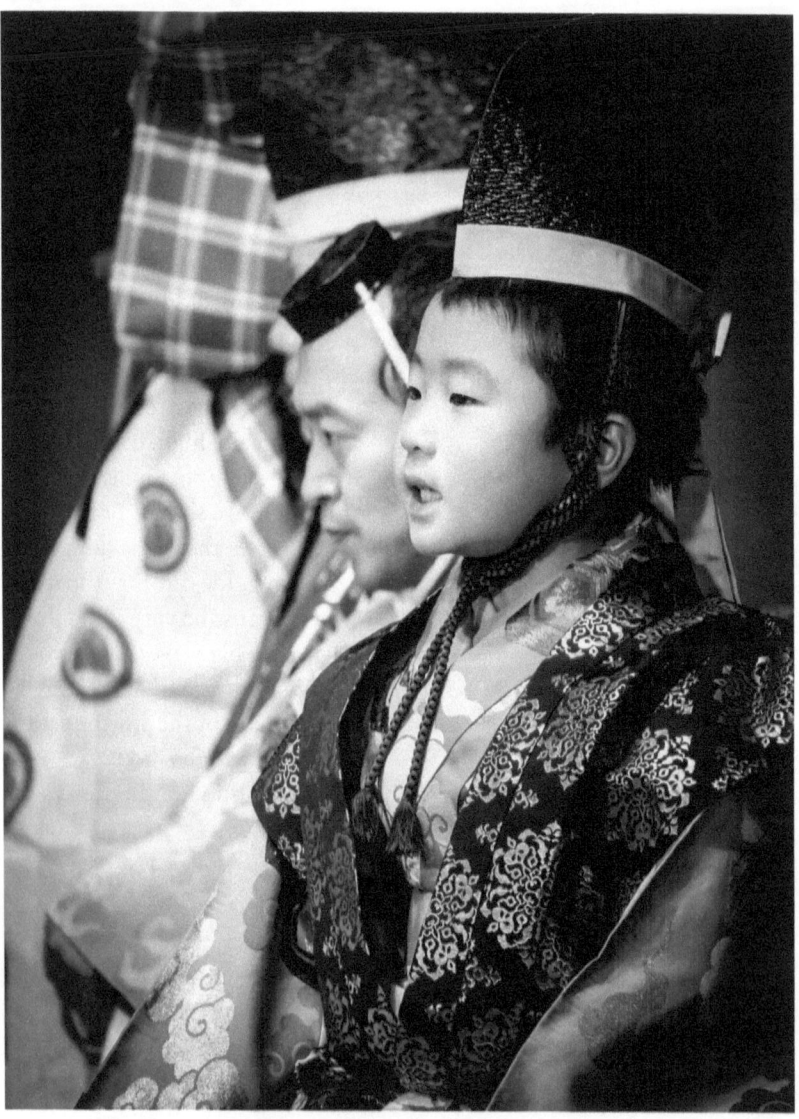

One of our samurai says that maybe we're being followed by ghosts. Benkei and the boatman tell him to be quiet because it brings bad luck to say that on a boat. But he is right. All the Taira soldiers who died at sea in the final battle come for revenge.

With my strongest voice, so that even the second-floor audience can hear me, I say we do not have to be afraid because if the Taira are dead, it was their fault and they should not have done what they did.

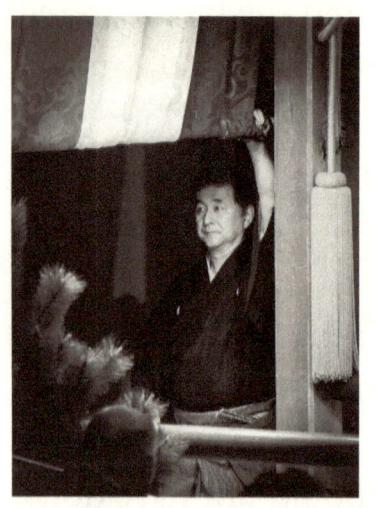

At that moment, my master appears in his new costume. He looks like a demon and has a big halberd. His mask is really scary and I wouldn't want to have a nightmare with him in it.

He is the ghost of Tomomori, the leader of the enemies from the last battle and he comes to take revenge so that Yoshitsune drowns in the sea like he did.

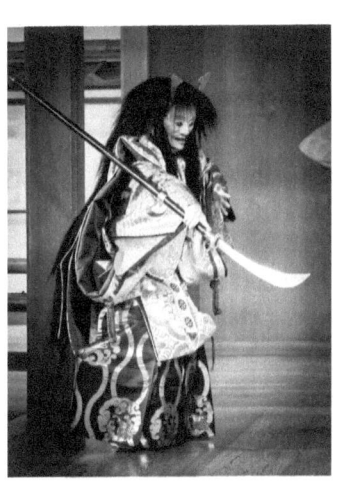
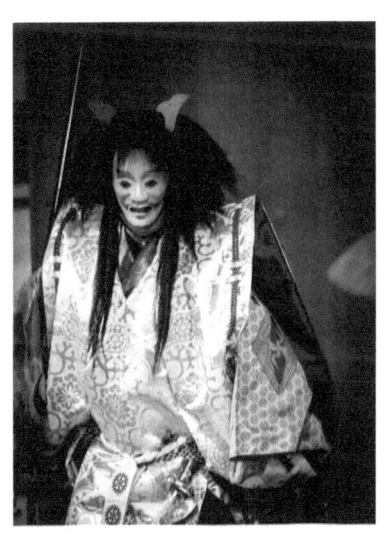

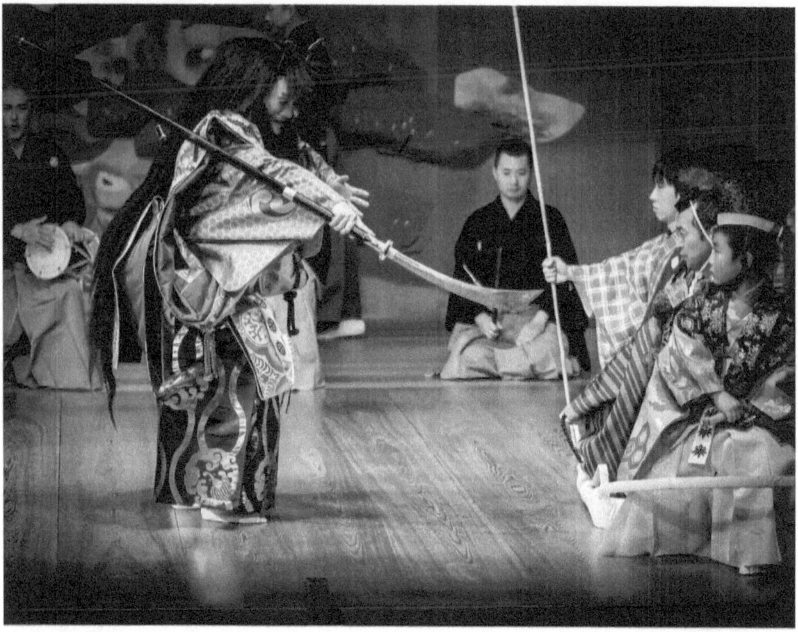

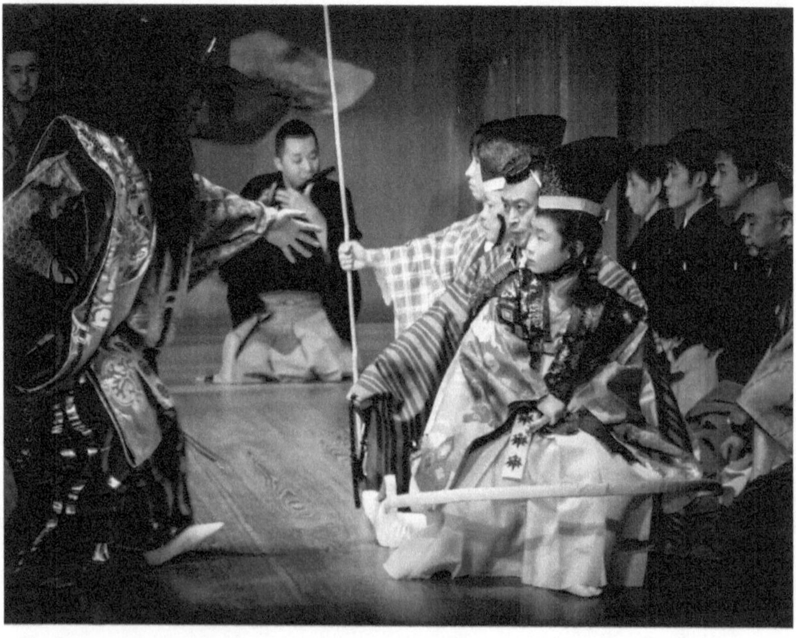

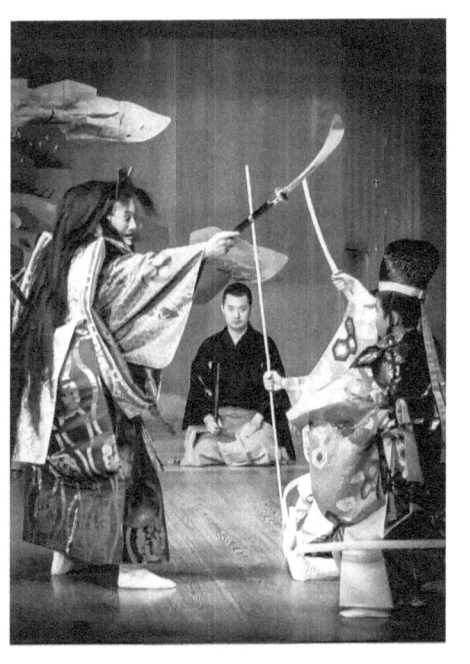

So I draw my sword to fight against him because I'm not afraid.

But Benkei tells me that against a ghost, weapons will not work and that it will be better to fight with prayers.

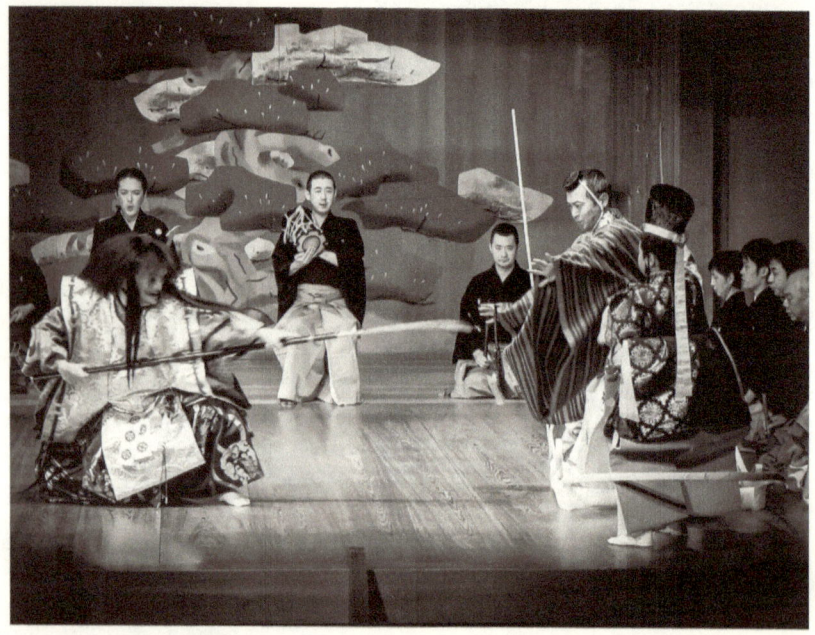

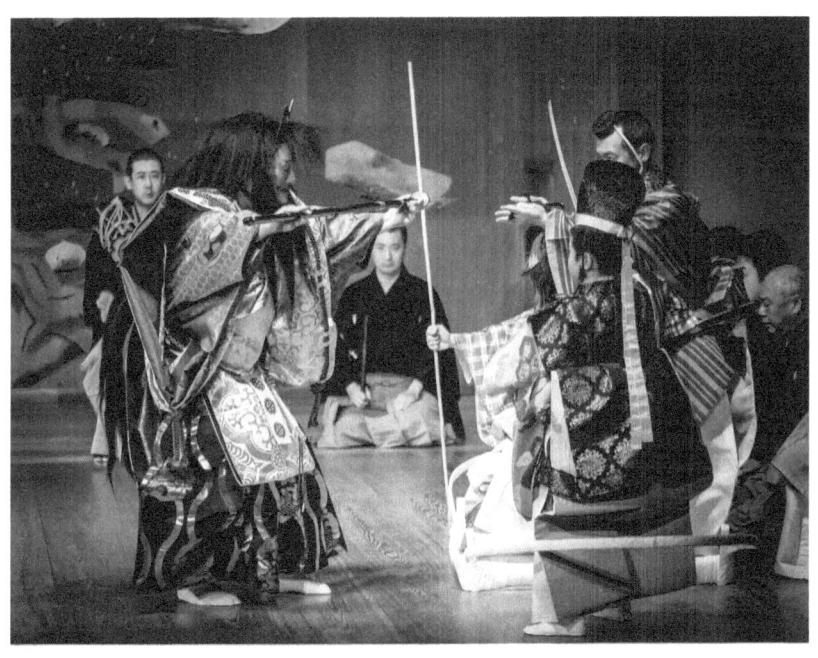

Because he's a monk that can say really strong prayers, he recites one that seems like a magic spell with a pretty sound from the rolling of the beads of his rosary.

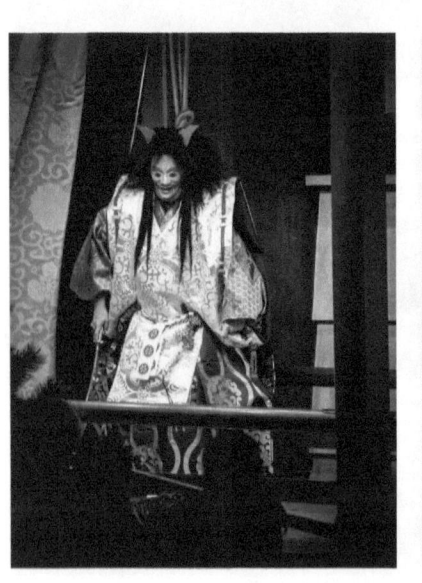 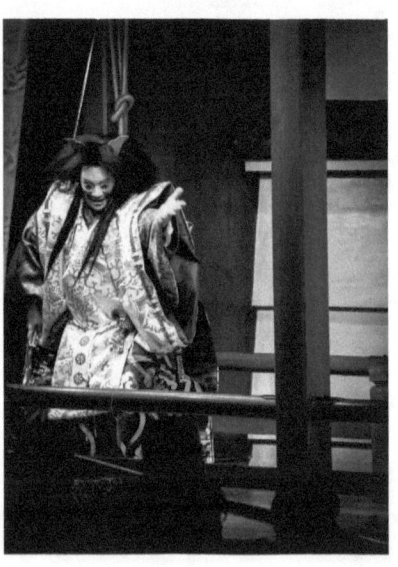

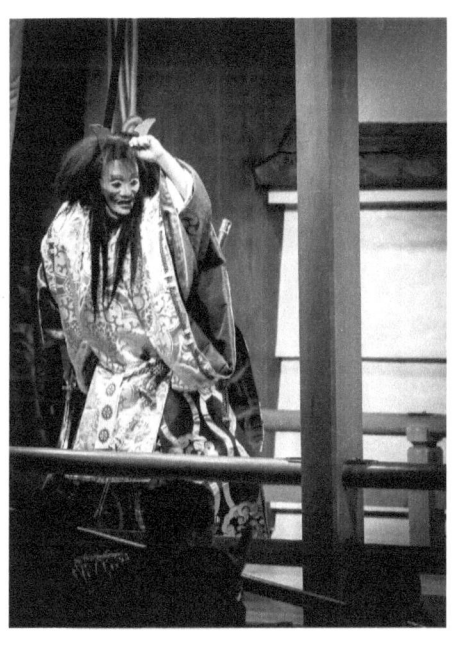

The ghost tries to fight against the prayer but it's too strong so he disappears.

Prayers can be so powerful!

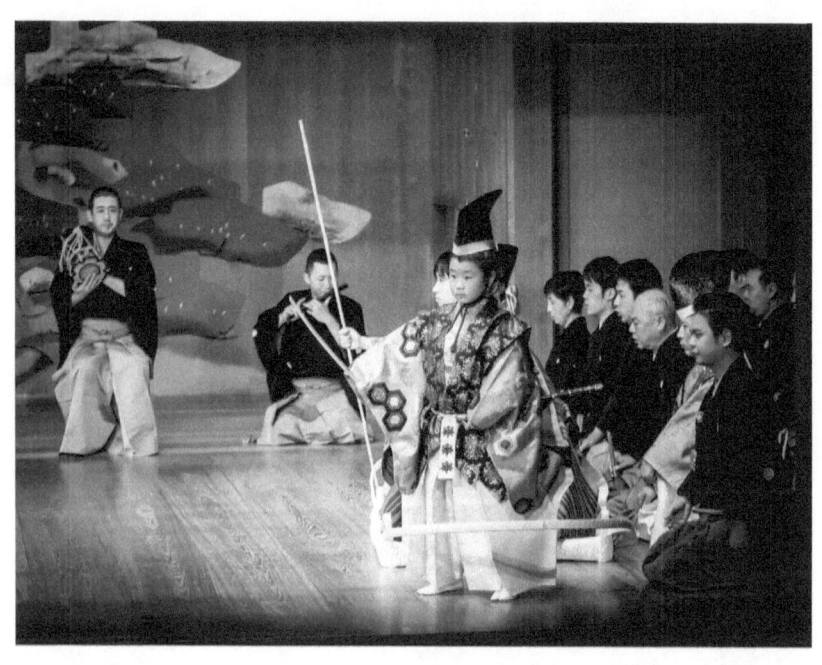

We've won.

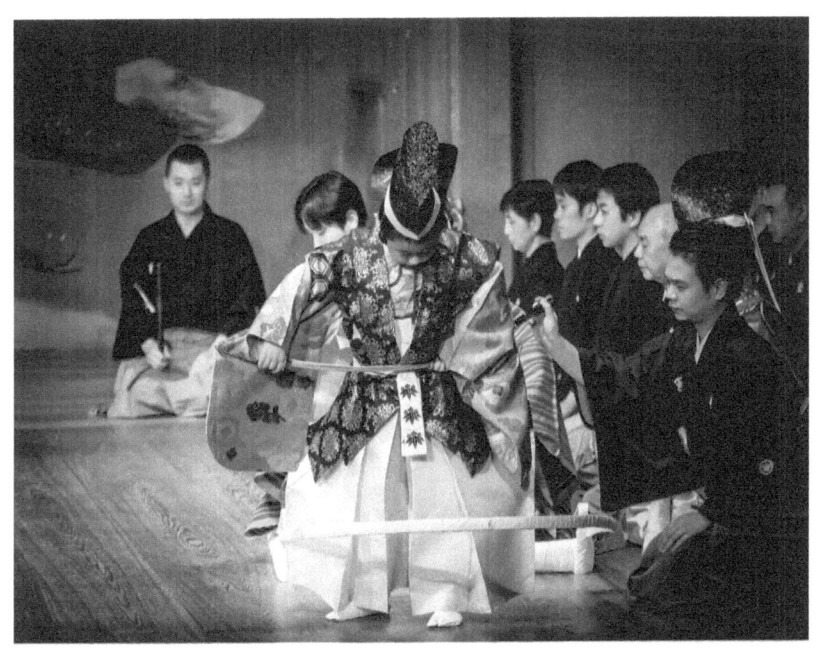

I shook my sword.
The storm has calmed down. We can reach
land. Everything is over.

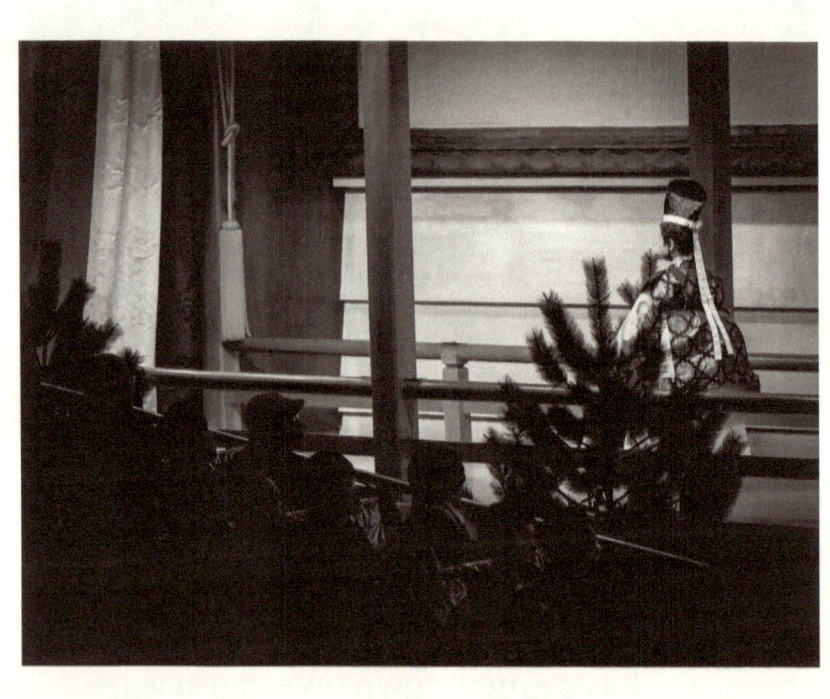

I leave the stage to the applause that begins only when I approach the beautiful curtain in five colors, which rises like magic.

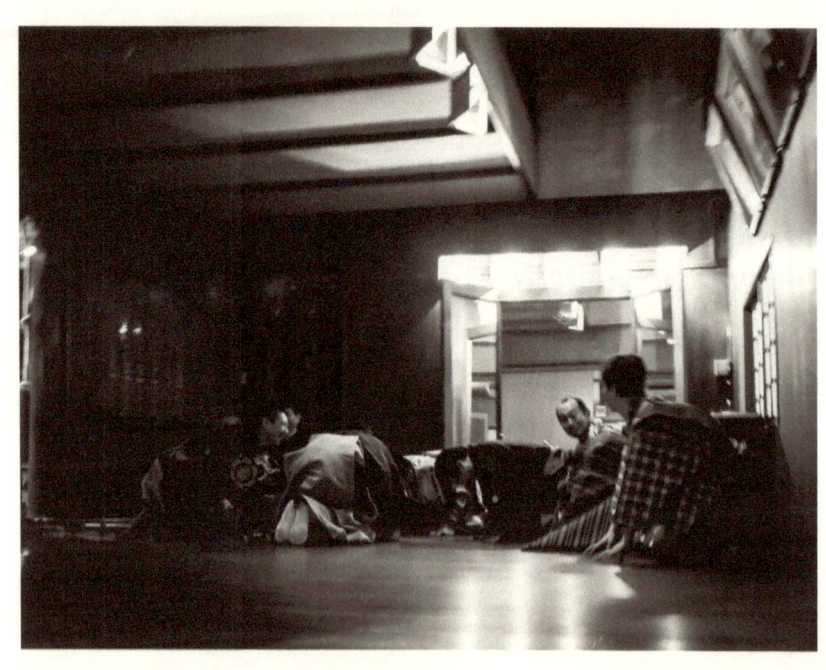

THE DAY
OF THE PERFORMANCE
It's over

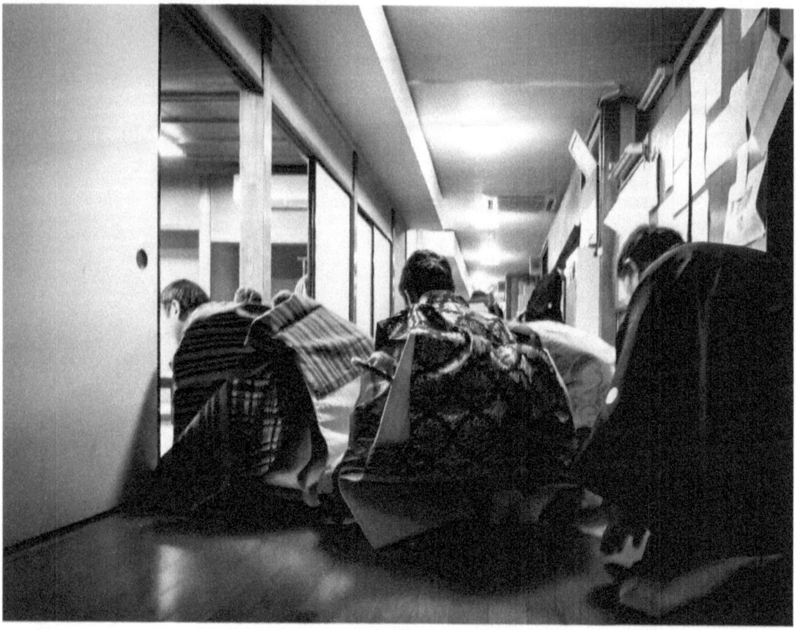

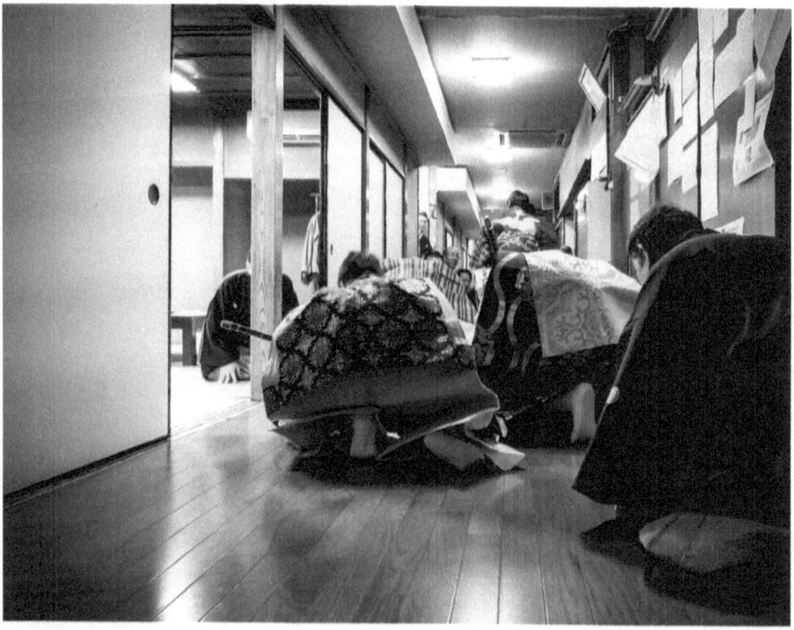

In the mirror room and in the big corridor of the dressing rooms everyone bows to each other like lords, thanking each other.

Everyone is happy, everything feels light.

I am proud and happy that I didn't make any mistakes and said my lines well, and that I didn't drop my sword during the battle.

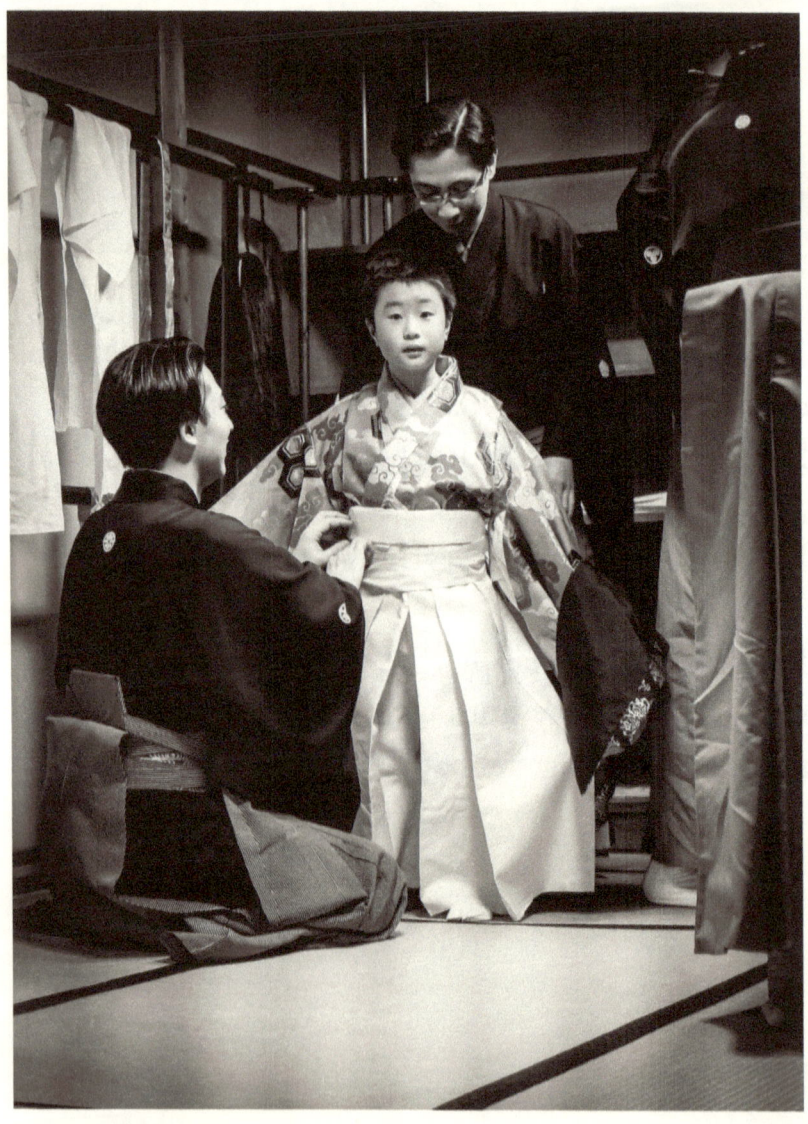

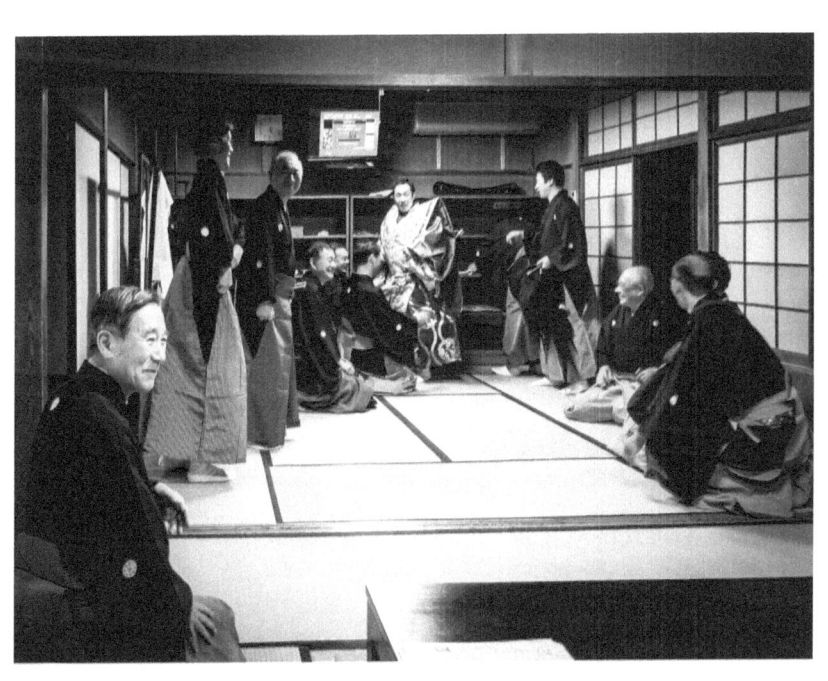

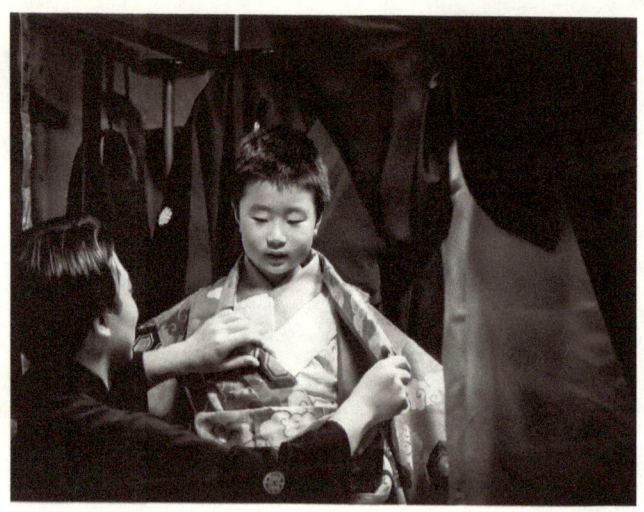

While undressing, I think to myself that it's a little sad that we rehearsed so much to perform the play just this once. But it seems this is exactly what noh is: the emotion of a single instant.

That noh is precious because of this. I feel older. My friends would not understand how I feel.

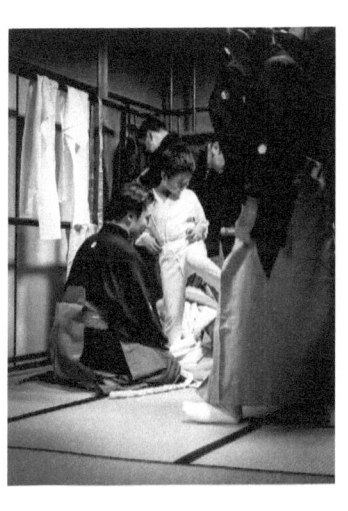

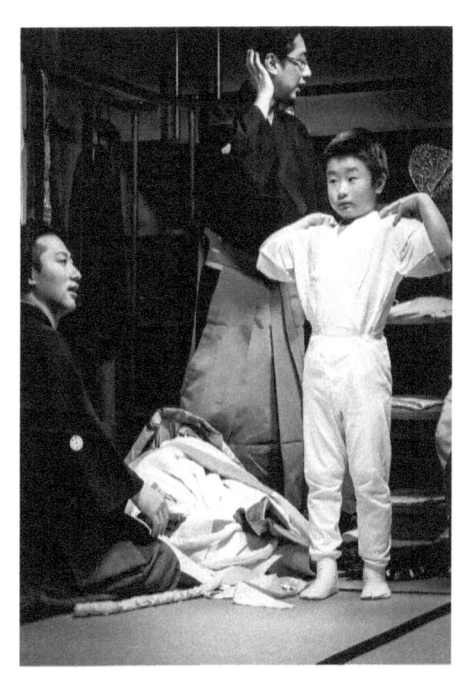

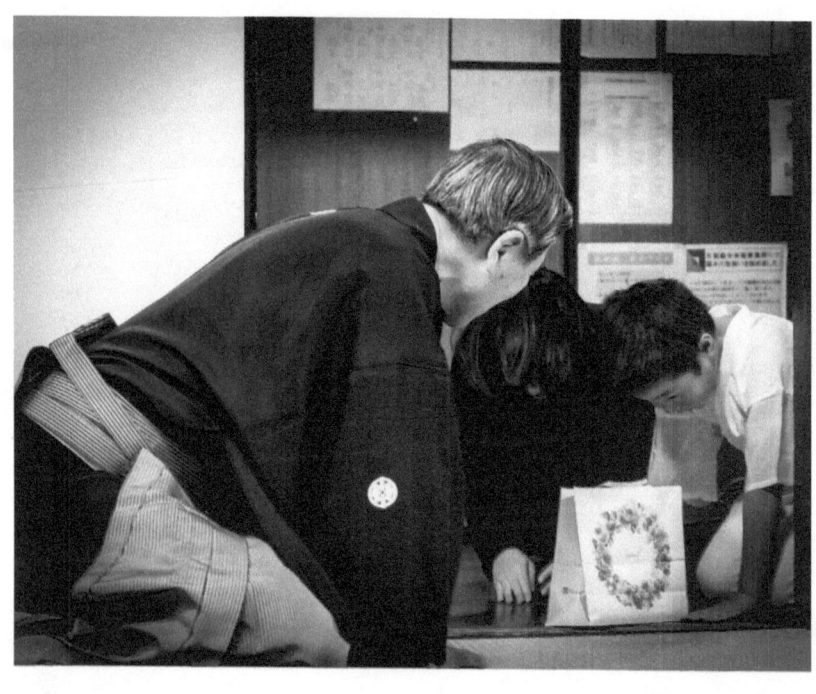

My master's master bows and gives me a bag with a present inside to thank me.

With Mom, I bow back.

And then I go to the room where the last spectators are coming out.

They look light, too. Like their hearts are washed, they're smiling.

If only everyone could come to see noh!

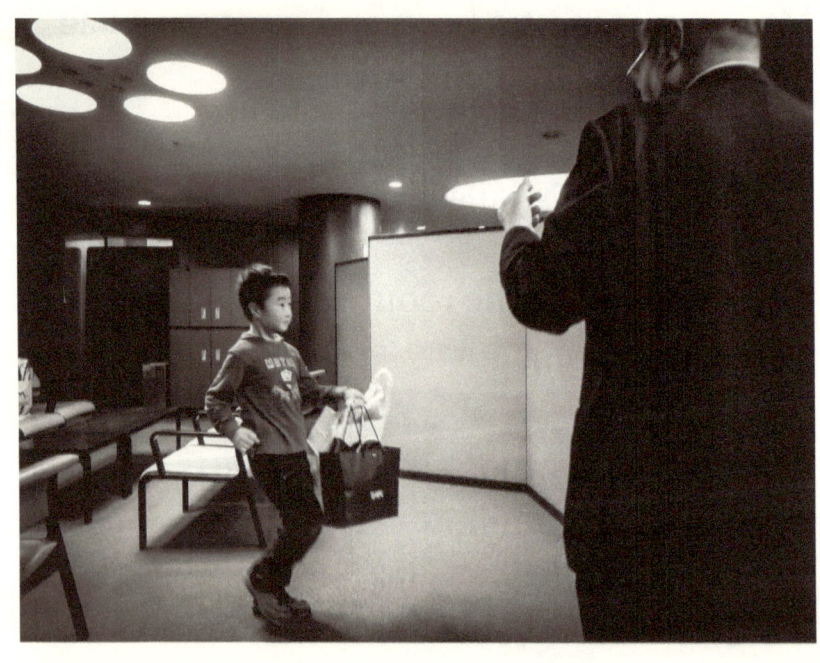

Acknowledgments

Funabenkei, Hayashi Teiki Nô, December 8, 2013, Kyoto Kanze Kaikan

松野 浩行	Matsuno Hiroyuki	Shite	シテ
上木 陽介	Ueki Yosuke	Kokata	子方
上木 佐和	Ueki Sawa	Mother	母
林 喜右衛門	Hayashi Kiemon	Master of Master	先生の先生
樹下 千慧	Juge Chisato	Uchi Deshi	内弟子
河村 浩太郎	Kawamura Kôtarô	Jiuta	地謡
河村 晴道	Kawamura Harumichi	Shite	
茂山 茂	Shigeyama Shigeru	Kyogen	間狂言
林 宗一郎	Hayashi Sô-ichirô	Jiuta	地謡
田中 義人	Tanaka Yoshito	Jiuta	地謡
味方 團	Mikata Madoka	Jiuta	地謡
河村 晴久	Kawamura Haruhisa	Koken	後見
河村 和貴	Kawamura Kazutaka	Koken	後見
斉藤 敦	Saitô Atsushi	Flute	笛
曽和 尚靖	Sowa Naoyasu	Kotsutsumi	小鼓
河村 大	Kawamura Masaru	Otsutsumi	大鼓
中田 弘美	Nakata Hiromi	Taiko	太鼓
江崎 敬三	Ezaki Keizô	Waki	ワキ
和田 英基	Wada Hideki	Waki tsure	ワキツレ
松本 義昭	Matsumoto Yoshiaki	Waki tsure	ワキツレ
國永 典子	Kuninaga Noriko	Jiuta	地謡
田茂井 廣道	Tamoi Hiromichi	Jiuta	地謡

田茂井 廣和	Tamoi Hirokazu	Jiuta	地謡
大江 信行	Ôe Nobuyuki	Jiuta	地謡
津々見 純	Tsutsumi Jun	English translation	英語翻訳
中村 知古	Nakamura Tomoko	Japanese translation	日本語翻訳
矢野 美穂	Yano Miho	Japanese translation	日本語翻訳